JAMES BRYAN SMITH

The Good and Beautiful Life

Putting on the character of Christ

HODDER &
STOUGHTON

Unless indicated otherwise, Scripture quotations are taken from the
New Revised Standard Version of the Bible, copyright 1989 by the Division of
Christian Education of the National Council of the Churches of Christ in the USA.
Used by permission. All rights reserved.

First published in Great Britain in 2010 by Hodder & Stoughton
An Hachette UK company
In association with InterVarsity Press
P.O. Box 1400, Downers Grove, IL 60515-1426

1

A CIP catalogue record for this title is available from the British Library

ISBN 978 0 340 99603 4

Printed and bound by CPI Mackays, Chatham ME5 8TD

Design, Cindy Kiple, Images: Paul Beard/Getty Images

Hodder & Stoughton policy is to use papers that are natural, renewable
and recyclable products and made from wood grown in sustainable forests.
The logging and manufacturing processes are expected to conform to
the environmental regulations of the country of origin.

Hodder & Stoughton Ltd
338 Euston Road
London NW1 3BH

www.hodderfaith.com

For my teachers

Dallas Willard and Richard J. Foster

*Scribes of the kingdom who have brought
us treasures old and new*

MATTHEW 13:52

contents

introduction

The great preacher and founder of the Methodist movement, John Wesley (1703-1791), was once approached by a man who came to him in the grip of unbelief. "All is dark; my thoughts are lost," the man said to Wesley, "but I hear that you preach to a great number of people every night and morning. Pray, what would you do with them? Whither would you lead them? What religion do you preach? What is it good for?" Wesley gave this answer to those questions:

> You ask, what would I do with them? I would make them virtuous and happy, easy in themselves, and useful to others. Whither would I lead them? To heaven, to God the judge, the lover of all, and to Jesus the mediator of the New Covenant. What religion do I preach? The religion of love. The law of kindness brought to light by the gospel. What is this good for? To make all who receive it enjoy God and themselves, to make them like God, lovers of all, contented in their lives, and crying out at their death, in calm assurance, "O grave where is thy victory! Thanks be to God, who giveth me victory, through my Lord Jesus Christ."

His answer is a beautiful and succinct description of the good and beautiful life.

But those answers are not what you might hear today. We seldom talk about virtue these days, but Wesley knew virtue was central to developing a vibrant, joyful life. How do people become virtuous? Wesley understood that the Christian gospel is the fundamental building block of the life we long for. We yearn to know and be known by God. But not just any understanding of God will do. Wesley describes God as the judge—God is holy—and yet he also calls God "the lover of all." We were designed to be in fellowship with a loving and holy God. Yet we cannot merit this on our own, so Wesley says he would lead his hearers to Jesus, the mediator of the New Covenant, a covenant of forgiveness and regeneration through which we become people in whom Christ dwells and delights.

And what is the religion Wesley prescribes? Not a religion of laws or ceremonies or mystical knowledge, but of love and kindness. Our world is badly in need of people who love, and it is hungering for people who demonstrate genuine kindness. We are so deprived of it that we are astonished when we encounter it. And what is the point of this religion? To get us to heaven? No, to get heaven into us. To help us discover a relationship with God wherein we enjoy God and are easy in ourselves. If we can discover such a life, Wesley believed, we can even face our death with calm assurance and the certainty of a joyful eternity.

The Apprentice Series of books, of which this is the second volume, is designed to do exactly what Wesley is describing. This book, its predecessor and the third volume have a single aim: to draw people into the divine conspiracy of love and transformation. The first book, *The Good and Beautiful God*, focuses on the God that Wesley described: loving, holy, forgiving and joyful. This book shifts the focus onto our own lives, hearts and character. It contains a method of growth toward a virtuous life of gladness and kindness. The third book, *The Good and Beautiful Community*, endeavors to help readers apply the principles of kingdom living into their everyday lives: in their homes, at work, in their communities and in their world.

HOW DOES JESUS THINK?

One of the central principles of the Apprentice Series is that we live at the mercy of our ideas and our narratives. What we think determines how we live. If we think God is an angry accountant frowning on us and would love us if only we are good enough, that narrative will be seen in how we live. Or if we think that being an angry person or hating our enemies are good things, then that too will be expressed in our day-to-day living. A lot of false narratives about God and human life are perpetuated in our world, sometimes even in our churches. The solution is to examine what Jesus thought, even before we look at what he did.

Jesus, the second member of Trinity, is intimately connected to God the Father and God the Spirit. Jesus reveals to us the character and nature of God, and his testimony is the best and most reliable the world has ever seen. So I believe that the key to beginning a good and beautiful life is to adopt the narratives of Jesus. I discovered that as I replaced my old, false narratives with the narratives of Jesus, my life began to change in many ways. I fell in love with the God Jesus knows. I began to see myself as someone in whom Christ dwells, as sacred and valuable. I started to treat people differently as I entered the kingdom, and learned that I really can pray for my enemies and bless those who curse me. Some of them even stopped cursing me!

THE FOUR COMPONENTS OF CHANGE

The mind and the ideas and stories that are imbedded in it are the beginning place for change, but transformation involves three other components as well. We need the practice of the spiritual disciplines, which are designed to cure the soul, not earn merit in heaven. Each chapter in this book ends with a soul-shaping tool that is designed to help embed the narrative of Jesus. I am convinced that while we can change by renewing our mind and practicing disciplines on our own, we find deeper and more lasting change within a community. We need others to help us see who and whose we are.

The mind, the disciplines and the community are foundational aspects of change, but the real change agent is the Holy Spirit. The Spirit leads us to Jesus, reveals the Father, exposes falsehood, offers correction, and gives us the needed encouragement that make growth and transformation possible. The Spirit helps us change our narratives by leading us into truth, enlightens us as we practice the disciplines, and binds us together in community. If not for the work of the Holy Spirit, transformation simply will not take place. But we must participate in this process. By serious reading and reflection, by practicing the spiritual exercises and by entering into community, we create the condition in which the Spirit can transform our character. Figure 1 offers a visual understanding of the relationship of the four components. The Apprentice Series is built on this model.

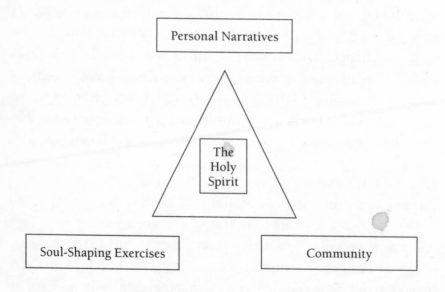

Figure 1. The four components of change

HOW THIS BOOK CAME TO BE

This book is the culmination of twenty-five years of learning from two great men, Richard Foster and Dallas Willard. Richard has been my mentor since I was his student in college. And I met Dallas and eventually served as a teaching assistant for a little over ten years. The idea for this book took shape soon after I began working with Dallas. He kept talking about the need to create "a curriculum for Christlikeness" for individuals and churches. His blueprint for such a curriculum can be found in the ninth chapter of his *The Divine Conspiracy*. Even as he was developing that chapter, I queried, "Can this really be done, Dallas?" He said, "Yes, of course." Then I asked, "Why don't you do it?" and he responded, "Because I think *you* should do it, Jim." No pressure.

In 1998 I began working with his simple blueprint for a course in learning to live as Jesus taught, and slowly created a curriculum. In 2003 I asked the church leadership board of Chapel Hill United Methodist Church in Wichita if I could invite some church members to go through this curriculum with me. They agreed, and I led twenty-five people through the thirty-week course. Midway through that year I began to suspect that Dallas was right. Genuine transformation into the character of Christ *is* possible.

Since that time I have led another seventy-five people through the curriculum, and the results have been the same: significant life change. One woman's response is typical: "What are you doing to my husband? He is a different person! He is more patient and more attentive to our whole family than ever before. I don't know what is going on, but you can be sure I am taking the course next year." This series also has been used in youth groups and on the college campus. Who is the target audience for this material? Anyone who longs for change—young or old, new Christian or mature Christian, male or female, it doesn't matter.

THE ISSUES ADDRESSED IN THIS BOOK

This book is aimed at your heart. Your heart is the center of your life and is revealed in your actions and solidified in your character. Spiritual formation is ultimately character formation. This book begins by looking at human life in general and asks, Who is living a good life? Chapters two and three explore the essential message of Jesus and who he is addressing. Both chapters introduce the available and unshakable kingdom of God and explain its importance in our lives.

The remainder of this book is an exposition of the Sermon on the Mount and follows Jesus' outline for how to develop a genuinely good life. Chapter four deals with anger, followed by chapters on lust, lying, blessing those who curse us, vanity, avarice, worry and judging others. Chapter twelve provides direction and encouragement for how to live in the kingdom of God day by day, with a specific focus on how to live one day closely with God.

I encourage you to proceed with hope and certainty that you are engaged in something that can make a positive difference in your life. I am confident that God, who has begun a good work in you, will bring it to completion. So move forward with the assurance that you can and will be changed, and as you change, those around you will see it and be inspired. May God change your mind, heart and life, and use you to change the world.

HOW to Get the MOST out of THIS BOOK

This book is intended to be used in the context of a community—a small group, a Sunday school class or a few friends gathered in a home or coffee shop. Working through this book with others greatly magnifies the impact. If you go through this on your own, only the first four suggestions below will apply to you. No matter how you use it, I am confident that God can and will accomplish a good work in you.

1. Prepare. Find a journal or notebook with blank pages.
You will use this journal to answer the questions sprinkled throughout each chapter and for the reflections on the soul-shaping experience found at the end of each chapter.

2. Read. Read each chapter thoroughly.
Try not to read hurriedly, and avoid reading the chapter at the last minute. Start reading early enough in the week so you have time to digest the material.

3. Do. Complete the weekly exercise(s).

Engaging in exercises related to the content of the chapter will help deepen the ideas you are learning and will begin to mold and heal your soul. Some of the exercises will take more time to complete than others. Be sure to leave plenty of time to do the exercise before your group meeting. You want to have time not only to do the exercise but also to do the written reflections.

4. Reflect. Make time to complete your written reflections.

In your journal go through all the questions of each chapter. This will help you clarify your thoughts and crystallize what God is teaching you.

5. Interact. Come to the group prepared to listen and to share.

If everyone takes time to journal in advance, the group's conversation will be much more effective. It is important to remember that we should listen twice as much as we speak! But do be prepared to share. The other group members will learn from your ideas and experiences.

6. Encourage. Interact with each other outside of group time.

Use technology to stay in touch; send an encouraging e-mail to at least two others in your group between meeting times. Let them know you are thinking of them, and ask how you can pray for them. Building strong relationships is a key factor in making your experience a success.

one

THE GOOD AND BEAUTIFUL LIFE

*"The meaning of earthly existence lies not,
as we have grown used to thinking, in prospering . . .
but in the development of the soul."*

ALEXANDER SOLZHENITSYN

One summer I worked as an intern chaplain at a retirement center. It was a pretty easy job. The residents were all in good enough health not to need constant care. They seemed to enjoy living together, kind of like a college dorm experience for people with gray hair, wrinkles and a lot of wisdom. I saw smiling faces everywhere I went. In our daily chapel a woman named Gladys played a hymn, I gave a short devotion, and we ended with one more hymn and a benediction. The rest of the day the residents spent thinking about their children and grandchildren, having tea or shooting pool. It was a pretty nice job. Sipping tea with grandmothers and shooting pool with grandfathers was not a bad way to spend a summer.

Mostly I mingled during social times, but occasionally someone would request a visit from me. One day my supervisor handed me a slip that said, "Ben Jacobs, Room 116, requests a visit from a chaplain." She looked at me and said, "Good luck with this one, Jim." Her tone told me that she knew I was up for a difficult afternoon. *What could be tough about this?* I asked myself as I made my way to Ben's room. I knocked on the door, and a deep voice bellowed, "Come in, young man." Ben sat in his rocker, with a shawl around his legs, wearing a blue cardigan and a button-down shirt. He had gray hair, a well-trimmed beard and very severe features: large, deeply set eyes and a very long, thin nose. He looked serious and important, and like one who would not be crossed.

"Good afternoon, Ben," I said, reaching out my hand to shake his.

"Sit down, son," he said, matter-of-factly, without shaking my hand.

For the next half an hour we talked about philosophy and world religions. I was not sure if he wanted to test me to see if I was intelligent and well read or if he just wanted to impress me. He certainly *did* impress me. He knew a great deal about very sophisticated matters in religion and philosophy. We engaged in a debate over which philosopher was the best. I suspected, however, that he did not want to debate philosophy, but I was not sure what he really wanted. After a while he said, "Well, you must have much to do. I will let you go now. Good day."

This time he did shake my hand, and as I left the room he said, "Would you please come back tomorrow?"

For the next six days I went to room 116 and talked with Ben, and each day he opened up a little more, sharing more about his life in bits and pieces. Then, on the seventh visit I discovered Ben's main intention. He wanted someone to confess to. Not any one sin; Ben wanted to confess to having lived a bad life. Surprisingly, his life, according to many, was really not so bad. Some might even say he lived well.

"I was born in 1910. I made my first million by 1935. I was twenty-five years old. By the age of forty-five I was the richest man in my state. Politicians wanted to be my friend. I lied, cheated and stole from whomever I could. My motto was simple: take all you can from whoever you can. I amassed wealth, and everyone was impressed with me. I had a lot of power in those days. I had two thousand employees, and all of them looked up to me or were afraid of me. Money was really all I cared about. I had three wives, all who left me either because of neglect or because they caught me in one of my many affairs. I have one daughter, who is now in her forties, but she refuses to speak to me."

Ben paused to look at me, to see if I was judging him. I wasn't. I was somewhat stunned. He looked so grandfatherly in his cardigan sweater; he looked nothing like the kind of person who could have lived such an ambitious, selfish, even sinful life. He went on, "I suppose you could say that I ruined my life, because today, I have nothing really. Oh, I still have a lot of money. I still have more money than I could ever spend. But that brings me no joy. I sit here each day, waiting to die. I have nothing but bad memories. I cared about no one in my life, and now no one cares about me. You, young man, are all I have."

EVERYONE WANTS TO BE HAPPY

Some of us are introverts, some are extroverts. Some of us like cats, others like dogs. Some of us like to take risks, others play it safe. Each of us is unique. But there is one thing that every one of us has in common: everyone wants to be happy. No one seeks a dull, lifeless, boring, meaningless life. I have never met a person whose goal was to ruin his or her life. We all want to be happy, and we want it all of the time. And we want it for those we love. Recently there was a poll taken that asked this simple question: "What did your parents want most for you—success, wealth, to be a good person, or happiness?" Eighty-five percent said happiness.

Ben wanted to be happy. He never set out to live a sad, joyless life. Ben did not decide, "I think I will make a series of selfish decisions in an attempt to ruin my life." He thought he was pursuing happiness.

Ben was pursuing happiness, joy, contentment and prosperity, just as all of us do all of the time. The problem is Ben had adopted a set of ideas about what success and happiness are, and they were all wrong.

He was simply obeying a false

Do you agree that everyone wants to be happy?

narrative about what constitutes a good and happy life. His dominant narrative, like all dominant narratives, dictated his behavior and justified the outcomes. No one ends up in a situation like Ben's all at once. It takes a long time to ruin a life. It all starts with the stories we live by.

To be sure, in our day there is a difference between begin happy and being joyful. Happiness is a temporary condition based on our circumstances. Joy is an inner disposition not based on external circumstances and therefore not subject to change. The old devotional writers, notably people like John Wesley, used *happiness* to describe the good and virtuous life. True happiness meant that a person was also good. Wesley said famously, "You cannot be happy without being holy." This is the sense I am using *happy* to describe the good life.

FALSE NARRATIVE: HAPPINESS COMES FROM FOLLOWING THE PRINCIPLES OF THIS WORLD

If you watch an hour of prime-time television, you will be subtly introduced to the world's values. Twenty minutes will be filled with commercials for various products, from hair care to hotel chains to tires. Indirectly, the narrative says something like this: happiness comes from sex, money and power. A bikini-clad woman stands next to a set of tires, implying that women will be attracted to a man who buys those tires. Or a handsome man looks very content as he enjoys his stay in five-star hotel. The point is clear: expensive luxuries will make you happy.

All of these narratives are false, meaning they are built on half-truths or outright lies. When we adopt them, they slowly destroy our souls. Ben lived by these false narratives. He amassed a lot of wealth, had a great deal of power and engaged in a lot of meaningless sexual activity. All behavior is based on a narrative. Positively, our cultural narrative can be stated a number of different ways: "Look out for number one." "You only go around once, so take all you can." "All is fair in love and war." These are commonly used to justify immoral or unethical behavior.

Negatively, our cultural narrative says, "Don't suppress desire; all desires are good." "Rules are made to be broken." "Don't be confined by your commitments." "Nice guys finish last." These were the narratives Ben lived by, which ultimately left him sad and lonely, captive to the memories of hurting others in his quest for "happiness." Ben told me that he was intrigued by Jesus but found his teachings impossible to live by. He told me that he assumed that if he tried to obey Jesus' commands, he would find life boring, constrictive and unpleasant. He assumed that Jesus would make him a weak failure.

HOW TO RUIN YOUR LIFE (WITHOUT EVEN TRYING)

In Romans 1:18-32, Paul describes how a human life spirals into ruin. Written nineteen centuries before the advent of modern psychology, Paul's assessment of the human person remains the most brilliant depiction of soul destruction I have ever read. Perhaps you will want to read Romans 1:18-32 in your own Bible, in its entirety, but for now I would like to summarize his ideas in what I call "The Six Steps of Ruin: The Process of Becoming Nothing."

1. *The turn away: I want to be God.* The first step toward ruin is to refuse to let God be God. To be more specific, it is refusing to give honor and reverence to God. Paul writes, "though they knew God, they did not honor him as God or give thanks to him" (Romans 1:21).

2. *The mind darkens* (*contra reality*). Now, if there is a God, as Christians suppose, then that God is the creator of all, the only being

that exists without a first cause, a perfect and powerful being. In short, if there is a God, we ought to honor and give thanks to God. Therefore, refusing to do that (step 1) is a step away from reality. It goes against the truth of the universe. Therefore, our minds, which thrive on truth and reality, become dimmed. Paul observes: "they became futile in their thinking, and their senseless minds were darkened. Claiming to be wise, they became fools" (Romans 1:21-22)

3. *Idolatry: We must have a god.* If we reject God, then something must take God's place: "Nature abhors a vacuum." Someone or something must take the place of God. We would like a god who would do a lot of good for us and ask very little in return. The solution: create an idol. Paul describes the next step downward: they "exchanged the glory of the immortal God for images resembling a mortal human being or birds or four-footed animals or reptiles" (Romans 1:23). Idols do not have to be little images; they can be anything we invest our lives in, in order to gain pleasure, happiness and a false sense of purpose. Here is the key: the idol serves us by giving us our desires, and we serve it by sacrificing our life energy to it.

4. *God leaves us alone: Wrath.* Unless we discover the futility of this existence and turn back to God, we are forced to push forward in our idolatry. Being rejected, God has no other choice. Paul delivers what I consider to be one of the most frightening verses in Scripture: "Therefore God gave them up in the lusts of their hearts to impurity" (Romans 1:24). God simply lets us be. God's wrath is his righteous stand against sin, which he cannot endorse.

5. *Pleasure is pursued at all costs.* Disconnected from reality and on our own, we must find a way to find fulfillment. Though temporary, the easiest route is through our bodies. Lust and gluttony are shortcuts to happiness. But the "high" that comes from our bodies (through drugs, alcohol, food, sexual encounters, pornography) has a constantly diminishing effect. Each time we engage in these activities, the pleasure decreases, thus requiring greater frequency or greater quantities to match the level of pleasure sought. Paul puts it this way:

"For this reason God gave them up to *degrading* passions" (Romans 1:26). The initial "lusts of their hearts" has now turned into "degrading passions."

6. *Sin reigns.* The final step is the worst and is a natural conclusion to the previous five steps. Sin and wickedness become normative, automatic behavior. When we reject God and consequently try to replace God with things that cannot satisfy, we naturally begin to reflect everything that stands against God, namely, sin. Paul offers a list that, though ancient, is descriptive of many today:

> And since they did not see fit to acknowledge God, God gave them up to a debased mind and to things that should not be done. They were filled with every kind of wickedness, evil, covetousness, malice. Full of envy, murder, strife, deceit, craftiness, they are gossips, slanderers, God-haters, insolent, haughty, boastful, inventors of evil, rebellious toward parents, foolish, faithless, heartless, ruthless. (Romans 1:28-31)

Each day when I pick up the newspaper I see Paul's depiction of the downward spiral lived out in the modern world: politicians using their power improperly, rape, murder, arson, runaways, gangs, drug dealers, prostitution and so on.

It all starts with that fatal first step, the same step by which Adam and Eve fell from God in the Garden: refusing to show respect and thankfulness to God. That step begins a movement away from a good and beautiful life, and ends in a life of sin and ugliness.

> How have you seen this downward spiral in others or experienced it in your own life?

SIN IS UGLY, VIRTUE BEAUTIFUL

Sin has many defenders and no defense. Sin is ugly. It is the opposite of beauty. When I see a man leering at a woman, it makes me cringe.

Anger can be ugly. When I see someone become enraged it is unsightly. Worry is unbecoming, and judging others is repulsive. When I hear someone saying terrible things about another, I feel ill. Pride and prejudice, deception and degradation—all are ugly. When I see these in others, it is clearly unattractive. But when I see them in myself, I am quick to rationalize and minimize them. Despite its ugliness and destructiveness, sin still manages to lure us into its illusion of happiness.

In contrast, virtue—not the outward appearance but the inner reality of a heart that loves goodness—is beautiful. When I see someone tell the truth, though it hurts them, it is lovely. When man treats a woman not as an object but as a person, I see beauty. A person who does a good deed in secrecy is a marvel and wonder. In *The Seven Storey Mountain*, Thomas Merton describes his life of sin and his eventual turning to God in his early years. He despised and ridiculed the word *virtue*, which had come to mean "prudery practiced by hypocrites." But Merton discovered that virtue, the power that comes from moral excellence, is the only way to the good life.

> Without [virtue] there can be no happiness, because virtues are precisely the powers by which we can come to acquire happiness: without them, there can be no joy, because they are the habits which coordinate and [provide an outlet for] our natural energies and direct them to the harmony and perfection and balance, the unity of our nature with itself and with God, which must, in the end, constitute our everlasting peace.

"Sin is always ugly; virtue is always beautiful."
Give some examples to back up that statement.

Sin is always ugly, and genuine virtue is always beautiful. Sin leads to ruin, virtue to greater strength. And this is why everyone, even atheists, love Jesus. Jesus was pure virtue. He lived a good and beautiful life, which he is calling his apprentices to live. A virtuous person is a light to everyone around them. I met such a person a few years ago, and he is still having an impact on me.

A LIFE WELL LIVED

In the summer of 2006 I had the privilege of meeting one of my heroes: legendary UCLA basketball coach John Wooden. Coach Wooden still holds many records that may never be broken. He won ten NCAA basketball championships, the last one in 1975. No other coach has had more than four. During one streak his teams won eighty-eight straight games. No other team has won more than forty-two. He coached some of the greatest players ever to play the game (Bill Walton, Kareem Abdul-Jabbar). He is thought by many to be not merely the greatest basketball coach of all time but the greatest coach of any sport in any era. To this day his former players call him, often once a week, to tell him they love him, to thank him for how he influenced their lives and to seek his advice in all areas of life.

Though he is revered for his success as a coach, his winning record did not make Coach Wooden who he is. During the afternoon I spent with him, I asked him the secret to his life. He said, "Jim, I made up my mind in 1935 to live by a set of principles, and I never wavered from them. They are based on the Bible and the teachings of Jesus. Principles like courage and honesty and hard work, character and loyalty, and virtue and honor—these are what constitute a good life." For three hours I wrote down nearly everything he said. I watched him as he engaged in conversation with my then fourteen-year-old son, Jacob, treating him as if he were the only person in the room. Jacob's eyes were wide as he stared at John's memorabilia: baseballs signed by legends such as Mickey Mantle, Derrick Jeter and Joe Torre, all saying things like, "To Coach Wooden: You are my inspiration."

John Wooden found the right way to live, and he lived it every day. He fell in love with and remained devoted to Nellie, his wife of

fifty-three years, when they were young. On the first day of basketball practice, he spent the first hour teaching his players how to put
their socks on properly. Not doing so, John said, would lead to blis-
ters. He was teaching his players an important life principle: Do
even the small things well. He told his players to acknowledge the
player who passed the ball to them when they scored. The practice
of pointing to the player who assisted in scoring started at UCLA.
Wooden told his players, "Discipline yourself so others won't have
to." "Never lie, never cheat, never steal." "Earn the right to be proud
and confident."

John has lived an amazing life. His love for his beloved wife and
for Jesus seemed to fill the room. He smiles infectiously, laughs easily
and is genuinely humble. He is glad to be alive, able to see his children and grandchildren, but he told me he is ready to move on to the
next life so he can be with Jesus and his beloved Nellie. John has
lived a wonderful life, "better than I deserved," he told me. But the
truth is that he has lived the kind of life we are meant to live, based
on truth, virtue and integrity, a life leading to true happiness. John
Wooden has lived a good and beautiful life.

You may have noticed that John was born in 1910. That was the
same year Ben was born. They lived through the same century together, witnessed the depression, two world wars, economic suffering and prosperity, and over a dozen presidents. They lived in the
same country, though on different coasts. Neither one started out
with a greater or lesser advantage, yet the difference in their lives was
stark. What was the difference? Ben lived his life under an illusion, a
false narrative about life and happiness, which ruined his life. He
lived his final days in fear of death. John arranged his life around
truth, around the teachings of Jesus, an accurate narrative about
what constitutes a good life. By following this narrative he lived a
glorious life, is content and looking forward to a radiant future with
Christ. Ben built a life on shifting sand; John built his life on the
strong rock of Jesus.

I want to be clear that God did not bless John because he did good deeds. John's good deeds led to a virtuous life, which is its own reward. God does not mete out blessings and curses based on our behavior alone—if that were so, all "bad" people would suffer and all "good" people would be blessed. But there is a life of joy and peace that only those who follow God can know.

Neither John nor Ben are normal in that both achieved extraordinary success in life. Both were exceptional in their own ways. But you and I are no less exceptional. Each day we make decisions that move us closer to a life of virtue or vice. We face decisions whether to be greedy or generous, self-centered or self-sacrificing, condemning or forgiving, cursing or blessing. While Ben and John were not average, everyday people, their souls are no different than ours. No matter who we are, we must choose the narrative we will practice daily.

> Have you met someone like John Wooden? If so, how did his or her life impact you?

JESUS' NARRATIVE

John Wooden became a Christian at a young age and built his life around Jesus' teachings. Jesus' narrative goes like this: "The good and beautiful life is created by doing the things I commanded, not as laws or rules, but as a new way of life." Jesus states this narrative at the end of his Sermon on the Mount. Later, we will examine that sermon very carefully, but I want to begin by looking at how Jesus ends his teaching. After giving the most profound sermon the world has ever heard, Jesus says,

> Everyone then who hears these words of mine and acts on them will be like a wise man who built his house on rock. The rain fell, the floods came, and the winds blew and beat on that

house, but it did not fall, because it had been founded on rock. And everyone who hears these words of mine and does not act on them will be like a foolish man who built his house on sand. The rain fell, and the floods came, and the winds blew and beat against that house, and it fell—and great was its fall! (Matthew 7:24-27)

All who take Jesus' words to heart and arrange their lives around them will be like a person who builds a house on a rock, never to be shaken, even in the storms and floods.

In contrast, those who refuse to listen and obey build their house on sand. When the storms of life come, they can be sure that their house will collapse. What words is Jesus referring to when he says "hears *these words* and acts on them"? The Sermon on the Mount. He is talking about his command not to be ruled by anger or lust or deception. Not retaliating or worrying, and not judging people. Strangely, many Christians simply ignore these teachings, seeing them as too hard or perhaps not necessary for the ordinary person.

This book is built around the Sermon on the Mount. The aim is to help Christians understand and implement the teachings of Jesus about things like anger, lust, lying, worrying, pride and judging others. What Jesus teaches about these things is simply the truth. Living according to his teachings leads to a good life, a life that can withstand the storms and trials we all face. Disobeying his teachings leads to a life of ruin. Jesus is not making life more difficult but is revealing that the way to the good and beautiful life is to obey his teachings. There is no other way. Either our lives conform to his teachings, or we fail to live a good and beautiful life.

MAPS AND LIGHTHOUSES

Years ago, Gordon Livingston was a young lieutenant in the 82nd Airborne Division, trying to orient himself during a field exercise at Fort Bragg, North Carolina. He writes, "As I stood studying a map, my platoon sergeant, a veteran, approached. 'You figure out where we are, lieutenant?' he asked. 'Well, the map says there should be a hill over there, but I don't see it,' I replied. 'Sir,' he said, 'if the map don't agree with the ground, then the map is wrong.' Even at the time, I knew I had just heard a profound truth."

Maps attempt to tell us the way things actually are. The closer a map comes to matching reality, the better it is. The same is true with our narratives. Some narratives are simply wrong. Other narratives, particularly those of Jesus, are exceedingly accurate—perfect even. We can easily tell the accuracy of the map by comparing it to the terrain it depicts. Lieutenant Gordon learned a great truth: if the map does not agree with the ground, the map is wrong. The ground is never wrong.

Narratives, too, try to guide us, to orient us, to tell us which way to turn. But *if the narrative does not agree with actual life, the narrative is wrong.* The false narrative Ben lived by proved inaccurate. It told him, "This is the way to the good life," but he ended up with a ruined life. The problem, then, is not with life but with the narrative. Jesus' narrative, in contrast, matches reality. No one has ever followed his teachings and been disappointed. No one has ever put his teachings into practice and found them false. His instructions perfectly coincide with reality. We will not find the good life any other way than by obeying Jesus. We must conform to his way.

One dark and stormy evening a ship with a proud captain was heading directly into an oncoming ship. The other ship signaled, "Turn around," but the proud captain refused. He signaled the other ship to get out of his way; after all, he was a famous captain piloting an important ship. The other ship signaled again, "Turn around—now!" Again, the captain refused, signaling, "No, *you* must turn. This ship is the SS Poseidon, and I am Captain Franklin Moran!" Finally the other "ship" signaled: "Turn now—this is the lighthouse, and you are about to hit the rocks." Certainly we are free to live our own way. So is a captain free to deny the light from the lighthouse and do what he wants. He is not free, however, from the rocks. Reality is what we smack into when we are wrong.

We should read the Sermon on the Mount this way. Jesus is not demanding we live his way in order to get his blessing or get into heaven when we die; he is simply telling the truth about reality. He warns against lust, not because he is a prude but because he knows it destroys human lives when unchecked. He tells us not to worry, not because it will give us ulcers but because people who live with him in the kingdom of God need not worry; it is a waste of time. Lust and worry, judgment and anger, retaliation and pride are never good or beautiful, and never lead to freedom. In fact, they are a flight from freedom.

We cannot find happiness or joy apart from a life of obedience to the teachings of Jesus. C. S. Lewis wrote, "God cannot give us a happiness and peace apart from Himself, because it is not there. There is no such thing." God is not being stingy and withholding joy apart from our obedience; there simply is no joy apart from a life with and for God. "God, please give me happiness and peace," we plead, "but let me also live my life as I please." And God answers, "I cannot give you that. You are asking for something that does not exist."

THE COST OF NONDISCIPLESHIP

Spiritual formation and discipleship cause many people to think about the high cost involved in developing a deeper life with God. Gone will be a life of pleasure, a life filled with laughter and fun. Entertainment, watching movies, eating delicious food, surfing the Net and playing games with friends will all have to be taken out of our lives. This is far from the truth. Those who follow Jesus do not have to live austere, sad and sour lives. In fact, the opposite is true. Christ-followers experience the highest form of pleasure, laugh with depth and enjoy all of the goodness life has to offer. Kingdom-dwellers are simply more discriminate about how they seek entertainment and pleasure. They trust in a good and beautiful God who has come not to rob them of joy but to bring them real and lasting joy, the kind found when moderation and boundaries are applied.

The idea that following Jesus' teaching will lead to a boring life is one of the most effective narratives employed by the enemy of our souls. Satan and his minions know all too well that real joy is found only in obeying Jesus' commands. But with a twist here and there, and the help of well-meaning but misguided religious folk, the Christian life can be portrayed as a holy bummer. The devil wants people to fear the high cost of discipleship. But in reality, the cost of nondiscipleship is much higher. Dallas Willard explains:

> Nondiscipleship costs abiding peace, a life penetrated throughout by love, faith that sees everything in light of God's overriding governance for good, hopefulness that stands firm in the most discouraging of circumstances, power to do what is right and withstand the forces of evil. In short, it costs exactly that abundance of life Jesus said he came to bring (John 10:10).

The question is not, What will I have to give up to follow Jesus? but rather, What will I never get to experience if I choose not to follow Jesus? The answer is clear: we will forfeit the chance to live a good and beautiful life.

ALWAYS WE BEGIN AGAIN: BEN REPRISED

Before the summer ended, during one of our many conversations, I ended up telling Ben that the only way to live was to follow Jesus. Ben did not offer much resistance to my statement. Jesus, he said, was brilliant. But he said it was too late for him; he had messed up his life and at the age of seventy-five was beyond redemption. I explained that redemption was God's favorite activity, regardless of age. During the rest of the summer we met each day, and every session became more and more joyful. We read the Gospels together and talked about mercy and forgiveness and the opportunity to change. By the end of the summer, when it was time for me to leave, Ben offered me a very special gift, a rare copy of an old book he knew I loved. Then he told me that he had decided to follow Jesus, had asked for forgiveness and somehow, in a strange way, felt that God had forgiven him. He showed me a letter he had written to his daughter, asking for her forgiveness. The book was a wonderful gift, but the change I saw in his life over the course of a summer was the best gift of all.

The last time I heard about Ben came when his daughter wrote to me, telling me that Ben had died at age eighty-eight. She said they had reconciled, and Ben had come to a saving faith. She said he spent his last years a changed man. Apparently Ben told her about our summer sessions and had asked her to pass on his gratitude. Ben did not live a radiant life, at least for the first seventy-five years. But he was changed and experienced a decade of devotion to God. According to his daughter, Ben died a radiant death.

When I think about Ben I think about how change is not only possible but mandatory. Every day we must begin anew. Though the past is written in stone and cannot be changed, the future is like wet cement, pliable, smooth and ready to be affected by what we do. No one is past redemption. All of us have the chance, no matter what we have done or where we have been, to change our minds, hearts and behavior, and to follow the wisest and most loving teacher who ever walked this earth. Each day, Jesus says to each of us, "Come, follow me." If we say yes, we can be sure that a good and beautiful day awaits us. And when we string those days together into months, years and decades, we will have lived a good and beautiful life. And that life is destined to echo a benediction of love for all of eternity to hear.

When in your past have you felt that you could change? What truths from this chapter could you draw on to inspire you that change is possible?

writing a letter to god

I would like you to write a letter to God that begins with "Dear God, the life I want most for myself is . . ." The rest of the letter will complete this opening statement (or prayer). You may want to acknowledge the mistakes you have made, but try to describe, in the rest of your letter, what a "good and beautiful life" would look like for you. Will it involve a major life change? Will it demand a new set of friends? Will it involve changing old narratives and habits? Feel free to dream big. Let God in on your greatest hopes.

Be sure to keep this letter in a safe place. You will likely want to read it at least once a year to be reminded of the vision you and God have for your life. Let it be a guide and an inspiration. If you feel comfortable, you may share it with someone you trust. If you are working through this book with a group of people, you may want to share your letter with them, but you are not required to do so. My experience has been that this is a great encouragement to everyone in the group.

REFLECTING ON YOUR SOUL-TRAINING EXERCISES
Whether you are going through this material alone or with others, the following questions will help as reflect on your experience. Record your answers in your journal. If you are meeting with a group,

bring your journal to remind you of your insights as you share your experiences with others.

1. Describe the letter you wrote this week and how you feel about it.

2. What did you learn about God or yourself through the exercise?

3. If you feel comfortable, share your letter with others.

two

The Gospel Many People Have Never Heard

If I had been asked, fresh out of seminary, "What is the gospel of Jesus?" I would have said, without hesitation, "Jesus died for our sins so that we can go to heaven when we die." Or if someone had put me on the spot and given me thirty seconds to explain the good news of Christianity to a nonbeliever, I would have answered, "God loves you. But because of your sin, you are separated from God and cannot have a relationship with him. Jesus died for you, and made provision for your sin. Through believing in Jesus you can know and experience God's love and receive eternal life."

Have you heard this gospel? Explain how it came across to you, and how you lived as a result of it.

I still believe this today. The gospel—which literally means "the good news"—of Christianity certainly contains this message. I fully believe that God loves us, that we are separated from God by our sin, that the sacrifice of Jesus is the only means of reconciliation, and the necessity of receiving Jesus by faith. I not only believe these things, I believe that they are essential and nonnegotiable. I learned those truths when I was becoming a Christian, and thirty years later I still believe they are true.

What I later discovered was that there is even more good news. In *The Good and Beautiful God*, I wrote about the importance of knowing that we are loved by God (chap. 5), forgiven by God (chap. 7), and raised to new life in Christ (chap. 8). These essential truths have radically changed my life. But I learned that this gospel is incomplete. I came to realize, thanks to some gifted teachers, that the gospel Jesus preached includes even more than being loved, forgiven, reconciled and given a new identity. I failed to know for over ten years of my Christian life that the gospel also includes an invitation to a great adventure, which I have come to know as "living in the kingdom of God."

To be sure, those other aspects of the good news (loved, forgiven, indwelt) were enough to help me live as a contented Christ-follower. But it was only after I discovered the "gospel of the available kingdom" that my apprenticeship to Jesus really began to make sense. Why did it take so long for me to discover this important aspect of the gospel? The good news about entering heaven when we die has overshadowed the equally good news that we can enter heaven now. The understanding of Jesus preached from many pulpits (even the one I stood in for years) is primarily that of Savior or ethical teacher. To be sure, he is both. But Jesus as rabbi, the one who teaches us how to live in the kingdom of God, is missing.

JESUS' NARRATIVE: GETTING HEAVEN INTO US NOW
In the following pages we will examine a lot of New Testament passages to see how prevalent the missing aspect of the gospel is. My aim is to let Jesus be our teacher, our primary narrative-giver.

Metanoia: *The kingdom of God is here.* After his temptation in the

wilderness Jesus was ready to begin his public ministry. Directly after his baptism Jesus began to preach:

> From that time Jesus began to proclaim, "Repent, for the king-
> dom of heaven has come near." (Matthew 4:17)

Presumably, this was the opening line of a sermon, a summary of his
entire message and perhaps his most provocative or memorable
point.

Notice also the phrase "from that time Jesus began to proclaim."
This indicates that he preached this message more than once. This
proclamation likely was included every time he preached or taught,
because we have no indication that he preached anything else. The
word *proclaim* was commonly used in Jesus' day for a herald who offered a very special word from the king. Matthew is telling us that
Jesus, the King of the kingdom of heaven, has offered a new edict
containing very good news.

Jesus' good news is summarized in a single sentence, "Repent,
for the kingdom of heaven has come near." The Greek word for
"repent" is *metanoia*, which means literally, "change your mind."
Most people think *repent* means "shape up"; thus they think Jesus'
proclamation is a *threat*. But it is an invitation. The kingdom of
God (or kingdom of the heaven) is an interactive life with God.
Jesus is essentially saying, "Change the way you have been thinking—a life of intimacy and interaction with God is now in your
midst." Jesus' hearers were aware that this was a gracious invitation, an offer so good that when Jesus taught it he often had difficulty escaping the crowds.

This was Jesus' first and only real sermon point. And because Matthew indicates Jesus proclaimed it every time he spoke, I have come
to believe that the kingdom was the primary topic of Jesus'
preaching.

Not only preaching but teaching. What was the content of Jesus'
teaching? The kingdom of God. Jesus primarily taught in parables,

and nearly all of his parables were about the kingdom.

> He put before them another parable: "The kingdom of heaven may be compared to someone who sowed good seed in his field." (Matthew 13:24)

> He put before them another parable: "The kingdom of heaven is like a mustard seed." (Matthew 13:31)

> And again he said, "To what should I compare the kingdom of God? It is like yeast that a woman took and mixed in with three measures of flour until all of it was leavened." (Luke 13:20-21)

It is much more difficult to find a teaching of Jesus that was *not* about the kingdom than to find one that is.

Jesus continued to teach his disciples about the kingdom of God even after his resurrection:

> After his suffering he presented himself alive to them by many convincing proofs, appearing to them during forty days and speaking about the kingdom of God. (Acts 1:3)

> **After looking at the Scripture passages above what stands out to you?**

Apparently the message had not changed. From his opening sermon to his hillside teaching to his postresurrection discourses, the subject is the same. Jesus preached and taught about the kingdom of God, and he expected his followers to do the same. In the Gospels, Jesus spoke about the kingdom of God *over one hundred times*. How can we have missed it?

WHAT JESUS' FOLLOWERS PREACHED AND TAUGHT

When Jesus sent his disciples to preach, he scripted their sermon to be exactly as his:

> These twelve Jesus sent out with the following instructions: . . .

"As you go, proclaim the good news, 'The kingdom of heaven has come near.' Cure the sick, raise the dead, cleanse the lepers, cast out demons." (Matthew 10:5-8)

It's the same sermon message Jesus proclaimed. This should tell us something.

What about the apostle Paul? Did he teach about the kingdom of God?

He entered the synagogue and for three months spoke out boldly, and argued persuasively about the kingdom of God. (Acts 19:8)

He lived there two whole years at his own expense and welcomed all who came to him, proclaiming the kingdom of God and teaching about the Lord Jesus Christ with all boldness and without hindrance. (Acts 28:30-31)

For "two whole years"—his final two years on earth—Paul preached nothing but the kingdom of God.

And in Paul's letters he uses the phrase "kingdom of God" or its equivalent fourteen times. For example:

For the kingdom of God is not food and drink but righteousness and peace and joy in the Holy Spirit. (Romans 14:17)

He has rescued us from the power of darkness and transferred us into the kingdom of his beloved Son, in whom we have redemption, the forgiveness of sins. (Colossians 1:13-14)

> Why are we unaware that Paul taught about the kingdom?

The kingdom is not something only Jesus preached and taught; his followers taught it as well.

HOW OFTEN HAVE YOU HEARD ABOUT THE KINGDOM?

After discovering that the central message of Jesus, his disciples and the apostle Paul was the kingdom of God, I wondered why I had never heard much about this before. I discovered I was not alone. Dallas Willard recounts the following:

> At the 1974 Lausanne Conference on World Evangelization, Michael Green asked rhetorically, "How much have you heard here about the Kingdom of God?" His answer was, "Not much. It is not our language. But it was Jesus' primary concern." . . . Peter Wagner . . . adds, "I cannot help wondering out loud why I haven't heard more about it in the thirty years I have been a Christian. I certainly read about it enough in the Bible. . . . But I honesty cannot remember any pastor whose ministry I have been under actually preaching a sermon on the Kingdom of God. As I rummage through my own sermon barrel, I now realize that I myself have never preached a sermon on it. Where has the Kingdom been?"

I was relieved after reading this. Michael Green, a leading expert in the area of evangelism, and Peter Wagner, the founder of the church-growth movement, were in the same situation as I was.

Martyn Lloyd-Jones, the great British preacher, noticed the same problem in his country:

> It is indeed very surprising that at the end of the twentieth century, men and women should still be all wrong about what the Gospel is; wrong about its foundation, wrong about its central message. . . . And yet, that is the very position by which we are confronted at the present time.

With as much biblical scholarship as we have available today, it is shocking to me that we have not heard more about the kingdom. If this is indeed the central message of the gospel, we simply cannot be wrong about it.

How did things get this way? I discovered that a powerful false narrative forced people to completely neglect the kingdom of God.

FALSE NARRATIVE: THE KINGDOM
OF GOD IS FUTURE

No serious biblical scholar would deny that Jesus' proclaimed the kingdom of God. However, many scholars conclude that Jesus was not talking about our present world but rather *an epoch in history that has not yet begun.* Obviously, the world as we know it is not running under the authority of God.

For example, Bible scholar John Bright says,

> The New Testament church . . . was confident that the victory of all the dark powers of the old aeon had been won in Christ, so much so that the Kingdom of God could be spoken of as a present thing. Yet it was all too painfully aware that the Kingdom remained an unconsummated thing of the future which had yet to come in its power. In tension between the two the New Testament church lived and waited.

Because Jesus did not establish a *complete* reign over all people and governments, Bright and others have concluded that the kingdom of God is "an unconsummated thing of the future."

While "the Kingdom of God *could be* spoken of as a present thing," in actual practice most seminary professors choose to put the emphasis on the future aspect of the kingdom of God, so much so that nothing much is taught about the present aspect of the kingdom. By labeling the kingdom as an eschatological (end times) reality that will come at the return of Christ, its role and value for our present lives is negated. This is a very big reason the kingdom of God seems to have been lost to most Christians.

There is no doubt that the kingdom of God has not been fully established. No nation, no state and no person lives in complete accord with the kingdom of God. My own heart and life is an example of that. I have moments when I strive and even succeed in living obediently to God and actually practice the principles of the kingdom. But I have just as many moments when I run the "kingdom of Jim" and choose to disobey the teachings of Jesus. Thus I pray, every day, "Thy kingdom come."

But this in no way means that the kingdom of God has not come or is not a present reality, or that it came in Jesus and left when he ascended. *The kingdom of God is a present reality that will be fully consummated in the future.* It is here and is as real and powerful as it will ever be. Everything Jesus said about the kingdom is true in our lives. Yes, one day it will be the governing power over the entire universe, but for now it is intended to be the governing power over you and me.

Jesus never said, "My kingdom teachings—especially all of those parables—are not applicable to you. They are about a future time when I come back in victory." While he did teach about the kingdom coming in its fullness, he primarily taught about the kingdom in the present tense. He not only taught about it, he ministered by its power. And by its power Jesus' disciples changed the world, not only in the first century, but in every century since.

WHAT ARE THE IMPLICATIONS OF THIS GOOD NEWS?

Just about everyone I know would like to have special powers. That is why we like superheroes who can leap buildings, stop speeding bullets or become invisible. Jesus tells us that those who live in alliance with him in the kingdom of God are endowed with a great deal of power—power to do good. It is demonstrated in the life and ministry of Jesus: "Jesus went about all the cities and villages, teaching in their synagogues, and proclaiming the good news of the kingdom, and curing every disease and every sickness" (Matthew 9:35).

Notice the connection: he proclaimed the good news of the kingdom and then demonstrated its power by healing people. When he cast out demons, it too was a manifestation of the power of the kingdom: "If it is by the Spirit of God that I cast out demons, then the kingdom of God has come to you" (Matthew 12:28). The kingdom was here and now and available, which Jesus demonstrated through his supernatural acts.

Lest we assume that the power of the kingdom was only available to Jesus, Luke 10:17-18 shows that Jesus expected his disciples to utilize the power of the kingdom in their own work and ministry: "The seventy returned with joy, saying, 'Lord, in your name even the demons submit to us!' He said to them, 'I watched Satan fall from heaven like a flash of lightning.'"

The kingdom of God exhibits the greatest power in the universe. Sickness and storms can be brought under its power. Demons are subject to a single word uttered from the kingdom. Paul stated it clearly: "The kingdom of God depends not on talk but on power" (1 Corinthians 4:20). So when Jesus invites us to be with him in order to become like him, he assumes that we will experience the same authority and power that he has.

HOW DO WE ENTER THE KINGDOM OF GOD?

In three places Jesus tells us what we must do to enter the kingdom of God:

> I tell you, unless your righteousness exceeds that of the scribes and Pharisees, you will never enter the kingdom of heaven. (Matthew 5:20)

> Truly I tell you, whoever does not receive the kingdom of God as a little child will never enter it. (Mark 10:15)

> Very truly, I tell you, no one can enter the kingdom of God without being born of water and Spirit. (John 3:5)

The first stipulation for entering the kingdom seems daunting: our righteousness must exceed that of the scribes and Pharisees, who were very religious people and highly respected for their piety. How can my righteousness possibly exceed theirs?

Jesus was very critical of the scribes and Pharisees because their righteousness was primarily exterior. They focused on outer actions (hand washing, sabbath rules) and not on the inner condition of their heart. The righteousness we need to enter the kingdom is humility, purity of heart and a desire to work on those aspects of our soul that are most important, such as integrity, gentleness, respect and mercy.

The Pharisees kept their outer life, which people could see, clean, but their inner life was filthy (Matthew 23:25-26). To enter the kingdom, we must work on our inner life. This is the aim of this book. In future chapters we will address issues such as anger, lust, lying and judging others. In order to live in the kingdom we must address these issues in our life. When we do, our righteousness begins to exceed that of the Pharisees.

To enter the kingdom of God, the second requirement is to become as a child. Jesus was fond of the attitudes and character of children. Pointing to a child in his midst, he quipped, "Whoever becomes humble like this child is the greatest in the kingdom of heaven" (Matthew 18:4). Children are innocent, trusting and have little self-consciousness. They do not naturally judge others or hate people. Those are learned activities. Love comes naturally to children. Of course, children convey more than innocence and love and trust; they can be petty and selfish and fearful. But children do *not need to be in control*. They have very little authority or power, and live each day in dependence and trust, receiving everything as a gift. And this, I believe, is what Jesus is advocating.

Being childlike does not save us, nor is it meritorious in itself. One can be childlike and be very far from the kingdom. Jesus is telling us that in order to enter the kingdom we need to have the trusting disposition of a child in order to experience the fullness of the kingdom. If we insist on maintaining our power and our control, we cannot enter the kingdom. The kingdom requires submission.

The third prerequisite to enter the kingdom is to be "born of water and Spirit." This is not a reference to water baptism. "Born of water" was formerly used to describe the birth, because infants live in the water of their mother's womb before being born. Every living person has been born of water. "Born of the Spirit" describes a second birth, which puzzled Nicodemus, who asked Jesus how it is possible to be born a second time (John 3:9). Jesus explains, "What is born of the flesh is flesh, and what is born of the Spirit is spirit" (John 3:6).

When I came into this world I was born "of the flesh" and "of water." But when I surrendered my life to Jesus, I was "born of the Spirit." How did that happen? The Holy Spirit had been leading me to Jesus for some time, and when I relinquished control of my life, the Spirit then infused my entire being with new life and new capacities. My love for God and my ability to understand the Bible increased. A few years later I was baptized by water, a sacrament that symbolizes that new birth.

Not everyone enters the kingdom the way I did. In fact, most Christians grow up in the church and are Christ-followers as long as they can remember; they cannot point to a moment when they were born again. Some may feel as if their experience is inferior, but in reality it is far better to have walked a whole life with Jesus. Either way, living the Christian life is learning how to be led by the Spirit: "For all who are led by the Spirit of God are children of God" (Romans 8:14).

What is it like to be so led? Jesus says, "The wind blows where it chooses, and you hear the sound of it, but you do not know where it comes from or where it goes. So it is with everyone who is born of the Spirit" (John 3:8). *Wind* and *spirit* are the same word in Greek. Jesus is saying that those who are led by the Spirit are not under a set of laws and rules. We are indwelt by a person far greater than a set of regulations. In order to enter the kingdom we must surrender our lives to the leading of the Holy Spirit.

THE HEART OF THE GOSPEL

Jesus' primary message was the availability, presence and power of the kingdom of God, which is the central teaching of the New Testament. The power of the church rests in the kingdom of God. The good news is that we are invited into this life with God. We enter the kingdom through surrender, humility, trust and a willingness to begin working on our hearts in order to become the kind of person God desires us to be. God is creating an all-inclusive community of persons whose hearts and character are shaped by Jesus. This can happen only in the kingdom of God. Fortunately, all of us are invited, regardless of our past.

After reading this chapter, describe your feelings about this new view of the kingdom of God.

play

Play is a spiritual exercise that can teach us about living in the king-dom of God. Many people think play is silly and not very spiritual. Play is actually very serious. By definition play involves randomness. We simply do not know how the ball will bounce or how our friend will respond in our make-believe world. Play cannot be controlled, no matter how hard we try. Sports teams try to keep the game under control, but that is impossible. Every "play" that happens during a game unfolds in unexpected ways. This is what makes play so entertaining.

Spontaneity is one of the spiritual benefits of play. We learn to let go. We relax, let ourselves become vulnerable and open up to what-ever happens. I was teaching spiritual formation to a group of twenty college students. One day I told them that instead of sitting in the classroom, we were going outside to play Ultimate Frisbee. Of course, they loved it. During the hour we played, many things happened that none of us expected. I stepped in a giant mud puddle. A shy girl turned out to be a great player. The best moment came when a dog ran onto the field and stole the Frisbee.

We play because our God is good. Grace is sufficient for us. God wants us to be full of joy, and play is a way to experience the good-ness of God and the richness of life. But many adults have lost the ability to play. Somewhere along the journey, life takes more serious turns: marriage, a job and children, and we find that we rarely play. At a retreat, I once asked thirty pastors what they do in terms of recreation and play. I was surprised to find that none ever played anything! One said he liked to work in his garden and wondered if that was considered play. I told him that if it nourished his soul, it was very close to play.

What are some ways we can engage in play? I have found the following list helpful. Perhaps you might want to choose one or two of them this week.

1. If you have children (or nieces, nephews or grandchildren), play with them! Do what they do (board games, hopscotch, even video games). Get down on the ground with them and wrestle!

2. If you once played a sport (tennis, racquetball, golf) but have not played in a while, dust off the old equipment and find someone to play with.

3. If you have a favorite hobby (collecting, painting, pottery, gardening) do it with a sense of play and wonder, not as work or something to be accomplished.

4. Engage in the discipline of wonder: read a book about something you do not know much about, or pay attention to the things around you.

5. Go to your local recreation center and sign up for a class: pottery, dancing, art, pickup basketball.

6. Rent a funny movie, make popcorn and laugh till your sides hurt. Laughter is a very special gift from God.

HOW DOES THIS EXERCISE RELATE TO THE KINGDOM?

Jesus told us we must enter the kingdom as a child, with trust, joyful expectation and very little self-awareness. Play is an act of self-abandonment: we stop taking ourselves so seriously and simply enjoy life. In one sense the kingdom of God is like a playground. Safe within the confines of a play area, with trusting parents overseeing their children, kids are free to slide and spin and climb and enjoy every moment. Because our heavenly Father watches over us, we are free to let go and play. When we play, we are training our bodies and souls to live with genuine excitement. That is what the kingdom of God is all about.

three

The Grand Invitation

I met Kevin about fifteen years ago at a small church I was attending. One day our pastor asked Kevin—who was in his late twenties at the time—to come forward and give his testimony. The only problem was that Kevin could not speak; he barely makes sounds. He had been born with Down Syndrome and a host of other physical ailments, including a reconstructed palate. As a result, he emitted grunts and snorts that only his mother could completely interpret.

The pastor therefore had to speak for Kevin, asking him yes or no questions, to which he would nod and grunt, and occasionally light up with a smile that said more than words could.

"So, Kevin, you just got back from the Special Olympics, where you won a medal. Was that a lot of fun?"

Kevin nodded furiously and smiled as he held his medal high. The pastor then turned to the congregation and explained how Kevin might have won more medals that day, but he stopped in every race to help other runners who had fallen or were lagging behind.

"Isn't that true, Kevin?" the pastor asked.

Again, Kevin nodded, but this time with a kind of shyness and humility.

The pastor then said, "Kevin, you are about the happiest person I know. To what do you attribute the joy in your life?"

Kevin pointed up.

"God?" asked the pastor.

Kevin shook his head yes, several times, then raised his hand as if to correct him, or to add to what was said.

"Something else?" the pastor questioned. Kevin grunted as if to say yes. "What else?"

Kevin then held his arms outstretched, as if he were Jesus on the cross.

"Do you mean Jesus, and his dying for you?"

Kevin not only nodded, but with great excitement started grunting and jumping up and down. He used sign language to say that Jesus loves us all, and that he, Kevin, loved us as well. He gave the pastor a huge hug, and most of us in the pews were misty-eyed if not downright crying. It was the best testimony I ever heard. And that was the moment I first began to understand what the Beatitudes are all about.

FALSE NARRATIVE: THE BEATITUDES ARE PRESCRIPTIONS FOR BLESSEDNESS

At one point while I was in seminary I began an intensive study of the Beatitudes at the beginning of Jesus' Sermon on the Mount.

When Jesus saw the crowds, he went up the mountain; and after he sat down, his disciples came to him. Then he began to speak, and taught them, saying:

"Blessed are the poor in spirit, for theirs is the kingdom of heaven.

"Blessed are those who mourn, for they will be comforted.

"Blessed are the meek, for they will inherit the earth.

"Blessed are those who hunger and thirst for righteous
ness, for they will be filled.

"Blessed are the merciful, for they will receive mercy.

"Blessed are the pure in heart, for they will see God.

"Blessed are the peacemakers, for they will be called
children of God.

"Blessed are those who are persecuted for righteousness' sake, for theirs is the kingdom of heaven.

"Blessed are you when people revile you and persecute
you and utter all kinds of evil against you falsely on my
account. Rejoice and be glad, for your reward is great in
heaven, for in the same way they persecuted the prophets
who were before you." (Matthew 5:1-12)

Jesus said that the "poor in spirit," "those who mourn," "those
who are meek" and "those who are persecuted" are blessed. Because
my most common narrative said we have to earn God's favor through
our actions (legalism), I naturally assumed this list was a prescrip-
tion for how to get God to be happy with me. Jesus seemed to be
teaching that those who had these inner attitudes (meekness) and
outer behaviors (willingness to be persecuted) were the truest of all
believers. As I meditated on the Beatitudes and studied each one of
them one by one, I began to believe that those who practiced them
were the Marines of the Christian army, the select few who were a
cut above the rest.

I was not alone in my interpretation. In fact, I would later discover
that this is the dominant narrative concerning the Beatitudes. A few
years earlier I had heard a pastor preach a series on the Beatitudes,
and each week he encouraged us to try to be poor in spirit or to be
meek or to stand up for Jesus, and if all went well we would experience persecution. Then we would know for sure that we were blessed.
This narrative says the Beatitudes are prescriptions for blessedness
or means to obtain spiritual wellness.

The problem is, this is a wrong interpretation. And of course, when you interpret a significant passage like this one incorrectly, a host of other problems emerge. After all, this is *the opening section of the greatest sermon given by the greatest person who ever lived.* If we begin in the wrong direction, you can be sure we will make a lot of other mistakes as we continue. Before we get to the correct understanding of the Beatitudes, I want to explain the context for Jesus' teaching. Failure to see the context is one reason we fail to interpret the Beatitudes correctly.

The main subject of Jesus' teaching is the kingdom of God. When Jesus arrived on the scene, everyone wondered when God would restore the kingdom to Israel. And there were five stipulations about who the kingdom was for. By taking a look at these five criteria we can more easily see what Jesus was saying in the Beatitudes, and how shocking those words must have been to some of his hearers and how exciting they were for others.

FIVE REQUIREMENTS FOR THE KINGDOM OF GOD

1. The dominant narrative of the Jewish religious leaders was that God had chosen the nation of Israel and was not going to invite non-Jews to the kingdom. Only those who were Jewish would be allowed to interact with God.

2. The recipients of the kingdom would be male only. In Jesus' day women were considered second class, or even worse, mere property. Some rabbis even said that women did not have the same souls as men.

3. The rightful recipients of the kingdom would be faithful keepers of law—holy and ritually pure. The kingdom was not available to someone who did not eat kosher or observe the sabbath—much less someone who was a known sinner (such as a prostitute, an adulterer or a tax collector).

4. The kingdom could be entered by the physically whole and healthy.

Sickness was a sign of sin and God's curse. The kingdom would not be available to the diseased, the blind or the lame.

5. The poor had been abandoned by God. Therefore the kingdom was for those who were wealthy. Even though the wealthy could be blessed by giving alms to the poor, the poor were not on the kingdom guest list.

Those who would enter the kingdom of God comprised an exclusive club: they were Jewish, male, religiously upright, healthy and wealthy. Jesus' ministry ran counter to this narrative. Jesus blessed the poor, touched lepers, healed and forgave Gentiles (even female Gentiles), and notoriously sinful females!

The religious leaders were shocked. By associating with known sinners and non-Jews, Jesus was saying, "You are invited." As L. Gregory Jones says, "because the cultically impure were welcomed at Jesus' table, they were implicitly included in a relationship of communion with God." The Pharisees grumbled and criticized Jesus for this, and Jesus responded with this little gem: "Truly I tell you, the tax collectors and the prostitutes are going into the kingdom of God ahead of you" (Matthew 21:31).

How could Jesus say this? Because he is the kingdom of God. He is a living, breathing, tangible, touchable, real-life expression and embodiment of the kingdom. When he touches or dines with people, they have come into contact with the kingdom. Matthew, a former tax collector, and Mary, a former prostitute, are in his inner circle. They have entered into the kingdom ahead of the Pharisees.

JESUS' NARRATIVE: THE BEATITUDES
ARE INVITATIONS OF INCLUSION

The broken down, sinful, ragamuffins of Israel flocked to Jesus. They tore apart roofs, climbed trees and formed huge crowds to see him. They knew he offered a vast treasure and was giving it away freely to everyone. Jesus was roaming Galilee telling everyone that God loves them, that God wants to commune with them and bless them, no matter who they are or what they have done, regardless of their gen-

—————————————————— der or ethnicity. And he was not
Think about a time you have just saying nice things; he is
been excluded from some healing people too. This was no
group. What was that like? ordinary man; God was with
—————————————————— him—and he proclaimed we
too have access to God! Those

not on the guest list are invited into the kingdom of God.

Now we can better understand what Jesus is saying in the Beatitudes. The Beatitudes, far from being a new set of virtues that further divide the religious haves and have nots, *are words of hope and healing to those who have been marginalized.* I will endeavor to explain what the Beatitudes meant to those who sat on the hill listening to this provocative teacher.

Blessed are. Each Beatitude begins with the words *blessed are.* Some translations say "happy are." Neither one of these does true justice to the Greek word used here, which is *makarios. Makarios* means something like "truly well off" or "those for whom everything is good." *Blessed* is a religious word to many of us today and is associated with being pious. *Happy* refers to temporary condition based on externals; it denotes a more shallow state of being. Today, the most accurate translation of *makarios* might be "well off." This translation heightens the shock value: "The poor in spirit are truly well off, because . . ."

There were other *makarios* sayings that Jesus' hearers were familiar with. An intertestimental book says:

Blessed is the man who lives with a sensible wife. . . .
Blessed is the man who does not sin with the tongue. . . .
Blessed is the man who has not served as an inferior. . . .
Blessed is the man who finds a friend. (Sirach 25:7-11, my
    translation)

All of these conditions are favorable. It is a good to have a sensible spouse and not to be inferior. These beatitudes make sense, and they do not shock us.

The same is true of the rabbinic teaching that those who mourn will be comforted in the hereafter. The more we suffer in this life, the less we will suffer in the next. "Be comforted," a rabbi might say to a person in mourning, "because you can look forward to a better life in the next." This too makes sense. There is justice in this: One day you will get your reward. Again, this teaching is not shocking.

But Jesus gives us a jolt. The Beatitudes countered the rabbinic teaching of Jesus' day. Jesus used words and phrases of and expressions similar to well-known rabbinic quotations, but in each case he turned them upside down. Alfred Edersheim concludes that Jesus' teaching not only differed from the rabbis but was teaching "quite the opposite," thus revealing "the difference between the largeness of Christ's World-Kingdom, and the narrowness of Judaism." Jesus' teaching is different and new.

When Jesus delivered his Beatitudes, I imagine his hearers gasped. He looked out at the crowd of desperate, sad, broken and persecuted people, and called them *makarios*.

Poor in spirit. "Blessed are the poor in spirit, for theirs is the kingdom of heaven." The poor in spirit have nothing going for them. These are folks who are in a bad state, and Jesus is announcing to them that even they are invited to the kingdom. Poor "in spirit" sounds like something close to being humble, but in Luke's version Jesus says bluntly, "Blessed are the poor," which is more difficult to spiritualize. Dallas Willard translates "poor in spirit" as "spiritual zeroes," meaning the kind of people who humans typically think have no place before God.

So the opening beatitude might read something like this: "Blessed are you who are feeling marginalized from God, who have nothing going for you spiritually—for you too are invited to the kingdom." Anna Wierzbicka notes that Jesus demonstrated great sympathy "for those who were marginal to society or outcasts."

The poor in spirit were in the crowd. Jesus was looking at them. They are the type of people this world overlooks. Jesus starts with them and says, "You are very well off. You are welcome in the kingdom of God."

The eyes that normally looked down in shame suddenly gazed at Jesus with hope and joy. Females, sick people, the poor, the second-class half-Jew, the person whose life had been broken by bad choices—all heard the good news. "Who me? Is he talking about me? I am welcome in the kingdom of heaven? It is here for me, now?" This was *very* good news.

Those who mourn. "Blessed are those who mourn, for they will be comforted." Those who mourn may refer to people who have undergone loss and are feeling overwhelming grief. It refers to a person "whose situation is wretched." Imagine a young woman who has lost her husband to cancer and is angry, confused and drowning in depression. Jesus is taking a very negative state and proclaiming that it can be turned into something good. People who grieve *in the kingdom* grieve altogether differently than those not in the kingdom. As Paul said, "We do not want you to be uninformed, brothers and sisters, about those who have died, so that you may not grieve as others do who have no hope" (1 Thessalonians 4:13).

In the kingdom we find comfort because God is in control, God gets the last word, which is heaven. Heaven changes how we grieve. We still feel pain, but we take comfort in knowing that we will see our loved ones again, and there will be no more tears. Laughter and joy await us. As in the first beatitude, Jesus says an unblessable condition can be blessed.

Those who are meek. "Blessed are the meek, for they will inherit the earth." Because meekness (or gentleness) is one of the fruits of the Spirit (Galatians 5:22-23), we think of it as a virtue, and of course it can be. But there is a dimension of meekness that is not necessarily a virtue. Scholars believe Jesus spoke in Aramaic, and the word he likely used for "meek" is *praus*, which refers to those who cannot retaliate when harmed. The kid who is not able to stand up to a bully is *praus*. He is not merely humble or gentle, but has no capacity to resist.

This is not a good thing to be in the eyes of this world. Certainly a person in this condition is not blessed. But Jesus calls this kind of person blessed because a *praus* will *inherit the earth*. This likely refers to land. The people in the crowd were too poor to own land (as most people were in that day). The landowners were often oppressive, charging large fees and asking for a lot work simply to live on rented land. So when the *praus* hear that they will "get their due," it was very good news. This beatitude promises that "the kingdom of the heavens enfolds them, the whole earth is their Father's—and theirs as they need it."

Those who hunger for righteousness. "Blessed are those who hunger and thirst for righteousness, for they will be filled." Those who hunger and thirst after righteousness certainly desire a good thing: righteousness. But these people do not merely desire righteousness, they "hunger and thirst" for it. Hunger and thirst are conditions of great need. These people are starving for something they do not have. They yearn for things to be made right. Perhaps the wrong is in them or is an injustice foisted on them. This is an admirable but not an enviable condition.

But as before, there is good news available to them. Jesus has a promise for people such as these: their hunger will recede. God will restore them to a new place where forgiveness and love will dominate. Jesus says to them, "I have come to make the world right, to make you right and to make all things new." That place is nothing other than the kingdom of God.

Those who are merciful. "Blessed are the merciful, for they will receive mercy." Jesus is not describing people who are simply *nice* in this beatitude. He is describing people who give until it hurts. I think of my paternal grandfather who ran a fix-it shop in small-town Indiana. According to people I have met, he was generous to a fault. People quite often could not afford to pay their bills, and he did not force them to do so. As a result, he and his family could barely survive financially. We all admire people who give of themselves for others, and most of us strive to live that way. When we do, however, we make ourselves vulnerable, and someone usually takes advantage of us.

As in every beatitude, the merciful are given a promise. Those who are merciful will receive mercy. In a society bent on revenge, being merciful is not often seen or highly valued. But God is merciful and loving and forgiving, and he will show mercy to the merciful. In the kingdom their kindness does not go unnoticed.

Those who are pure in heart. "Blessed are the pure in heart, for they will see God." Most of us strive to be pure in heart. We live in a broken and depraved world, and we find a lot of darkness in our own hearts. In "As the Ruin Falls," C. S. Lewis wrote, "I have never had a selfless thought." Our motives are mixed and often selfish. We would like to speak without guile, to love with pure intentions and to serve with the right motives. But it eludes us. We find that we are a mixture of good and evil. We long to do right, just as the person who hungers for righteousness, but in this case our yearning is to be pure so that we can see God.

This beatitude is built on Psalm 24:

Who shall ascend the hill of the LORD?
    And who shall stand in his holy place?
Those who have clean hands and pure hearts,
    who do not lift up their souls to what is false,
    and do not swear deceitfully (Psalm 24:3-4)

Who can stand in God's presence? Those who "have clean hands and pure hearts."

Jesus is addressing people whose longing is never fulfilled. They are never perfect enough. God seems to elude them. They grit their teeth and resolve to do better because they want to see God so badly. Jesus informs them they will see God. Of course, he knows that this is not just a future promise. When they look at Jesus they see God. *They have found what they have been seeking and are truly well off.*

Those who are peacemakers. "Blessed are the peacemakers, for they will be called children of God." Peacemakers stand amid those who are fighting; they are "caught in the middle." A police officer allowed me to ride with him for about three hours, which was about all I could handle. During that time he dealt with several people who had or were in the process of committing crimes. The officer had to step in and use as much force as necessary to deal with people who were less than polite.

The officer is a peacemaker. He goes where we would not, and does it because he believes in protecting the innocent. This is what Jesus is addressing in this beatitude. Using force to make an enemy bow is not peacemaking. Peacemakers are willing to suffer and even die for the cause of peace. Peacemakers will be called the sons and daughters of God because they do what their heavenly Father does. Our God is a peacemaker, and human peacemakers resemble him.

Those who are persecuted. "Blessed are those who are persecuted for righteousness' sake, for theirs is the kingdom of heaven." The last to be blessed are the persecuted. We rightly esteem those willing to suffer for their faith. I read with awe the stories of men and women who accept martyrdom with courage and even joy. But this certainly is not valued in this world. We are easily offended by a slight criticism. We want everyone in it to think well of us. We want praise, not persecution.

> Which of the Beatitudes do you most relate to? Describe the negative and positive.

Jesus observes that those who pursue righteousness are going against the grain of society, and that will result in persecution. Following Jesus is dangerous—if we lead the kind of life he calls us to. When we choose to fight for justice and peace or not to lie or judge others, we will face backlash.

The promise in the last beatitude is the same as in the first: "for theirs is the kingdom of heaven." When we align ourselves with Jesus and observe his ways, we are in the kingdom.

BLESSED BECAUSE THEY ARE POOR?

The people mentioned in the Beatitudes are not blessed because they are in those conditions. They are blessed *because of Jesus*. They have hope because the kingdom is available to even them. Their character traits are not highly valued by the world. As my friend and colleague Matt Johnson put it so well, the Beatitudes "are characteristics that won't lead to power, prestige, or possessions." Jesus opens the Sermon on the Mount with the radical teaching that these people are invited to the great banquet.

People are not blessed merely because they are poor in spirit. The condition is not important. What is important is that these people are not cut off from God. Their life situation does not prevent them from entering the kingdom. Most of Jesus' teaching went against the grain of dominant narratives ("You have heard that it was said. . . . But I say to you . . ."). The Beatitudes are not different. The life circumstances Jesus called blessed are commonly thought to be anything but that. And the Beatitudes are radical because they teach that these people have the same access to the kingdom as the rich and happy.

What if I am not on the list? If I am not poor, is the kingdom of heaven mine as well? If I am happy, is there any comfort for me? Of course. Jesus does not include the rich in spirit because everyone already knows they are blessed. But they did not know that people who were poor in spirit had equal opportunity in the kingdom.

WARNING TO THE RICH AND POWERFUL

In Luke's version of the Beatitudes Jesus offers a warning that is worth heeding, perhaps especially today:

> But woe to you who are rich,
>> for you have received your consolation.
> Woe to you who are full now,
>> for you will be hungry.
> Woe to you who are laughing now,
>> for you will mourn and weep. (Luke 6:24-25)

Jesus warns them not because God does not accept rich, satisfied or happy people, but because rich, satisfied and happy people often think they have no need for God.

Wealth, power and possessions can easily numb us to our need for God and make us overlook the needs of others. The wealthy must be concerned for the poor. Eating gourmet meals when others have nothing to eat should cause us to reflect a bit. Pursuing pleasure in a world with so much pain creates uneasiness in those who follow Jesus. God is not against fine food or having fun, but we ought to think deeply about our decisions—what and how much we buy, what is truly important—because we live in a world of great disparity.

Have you seen this in your life or in the lives of others?

The solution is not to close out our bank account and hand it all to a charitable foundation or to stop eating. Jesus' stern warning is born of love. He knows that we try to find solace in our wealth and fulfillment in our bellies. And we confuse fleeting pleasure with joy. When all is well in the kingdom of this world, we are tempted to think we have no need of the kingdom of God. When the wealthy, full and happy share with those who have less, they find satisfaction in things that truly satisfy.

THE BLESSED SHALL BLESS

In the Beatitudes Jesus invites the down and out to live in fellowship with him. He invites them to the kingdom of God. Jesus *is* the kingdom of God in the flesh. He is Immanuel, God with us. He does not introduce people to a concept or a religious idea, he invites them into a vibrant, interactive relationship with himself. And Jesus embodies and fulfills the Beatititudes. He was poor in spirit, meek and pure in heart. He hungered for righteousness, mourned for Jerusalem and wept for Lazarus. And he was persecuted. Pope Benedict XVI explains this beautifully:

> The Beatitudes, spoken with the community of Jesus' disciples in view, are paradoxes—the standards of the world are turned upside down as soon as things are seen in their right perspective, which is to say, in terms of God's values, so different from those of the world. It is precisely those who are poor in worldly terms, those thought of as lost souls, who are truly fortunate ones, the blessed, who have every reason to rejoice and exult in the midst of their suffering. The Beatitudes are promises resplendent with the new image of the world and of man inaugurated by Jesus.

Jesus inaugurated and exemplified this upside-down world through his life and in his teachings.

Those who are in Christ become *living beatitudes*, walking, talking blessings to the world. Immediately after the Beatitudes Jesus says, "*You* are the salt of the earth. . . . *You* are the light of the world. . . . [L]et your light shine before others, so that they may see your good works and give glory to your Father in heaven" (Matthew 5:13-16). Jesus not only invited these ragtag people into the kingdom but calls them the salt of the earth and the light of the world. Those who live with Jesus in his kingdom are destined to be witnesses for another way of life, where the last are first and the greatest are least.

When I heard Kevin speak in church I was watching a *living beatitude*. His condition seemed unblessable in the kingdom of this world. According to society's values, he has nothing going for him. He is marginalized, ostracized and neglected. No one would choose his situation. And yet he is welcomed, esteemed and valued in the God's kingdom, which is why he smiled. It is also why he never competes—there is no competition in the kingdom. We are all on the same team, all members of the same family, where everyone wins.

Kevin lets his light shine in our congregation through his compassion for people who have lost their spouses. Many people in this congregation were elderly, and every few weeks one of our members would pass away. Kevin would look the surviving spouse in the eyes, touch his finger to his eye and run it down his cheek, to indicate tears. Then he would put his hands together in a posture of prayer. Finally, he would give them a big hug and walk away. Without words he conveyed, "I am sad with you. I am praying for you. I love you." The people who receive his blessing say the same thing: "Of all the people who tried to help me after I lost my spouse, Kevin helped me the most with my grief." Kevin, rejected by the world but one in whom Christ dwells, brings comfort to those who mourn.

How has God used you, especially in your weaknesses?

SOUL TRAINING

Hospitality

The Beatitudes invite marginalized people into the kingdom of God, and hospitality can help us practice this essential aspect of the kingdom: God cares deeply about those who are left out. The kingdom is inclusive, but the world we live in is exclusive. And if we are honest, we likely are more exclusive than inclusive in our own lives. The authors of *Radical Hospitality* note:

> When we speak of hospitality we are always addressing issues of inclusion and exclusion. Each of us makes choices about who will and who will not be included in our lives. . . . Our entire culture excludes many people. If you are in a wheelchair, for example, you are excluded because there are places you can't go. If you are very young, if you are very old, you are excluded. In high school you can be excluded if you don't wear the right shoes or listen to the right music. Women are excluded, as are people of color, and those who practice a different religion from our own. . . . The poor are always excluded; they are our embarrassing little American secret.

Living in the kingdom of God involves loving others, because our King is a God of love. Living in the kingdom of God involves forgiving others, because our King is a God of forgiveness. In the same manner, living in the kingdom of God involves hospitality—*inviting and including others*—because our King is a God of hospitality.

Practicing hospitality makes us vulnerable, and this is why we refrain from it. As long as I spend time with people I know, people who are like me, I feel relatively safe. But if I open myself or my home to someone outside of my comfort zone, I may encounter something I do not like. This does not mean that we put ourselves in situations of risk: "Opening yourselves to the stranger is not equivalent to leaving your door unlocked and bringing strangers into your home. Hospitality does not mean you ignore obvious threats to personal safety."

That said, we will still likely feel a bit uncomfortable. When we open ourselves to someone else we become vulnerable: What if they reject my hospitality? What if the situation becomes awkward? Knowing this is going to happen will help alleviate those fears. Simply remind yourself that feeling a bit uncomfortable is normal. Once you do it a few times, those fears will diminish.

Try to do two or three of the following suggestions this week.

- Reach out to someone outside of your comfort zone. Ask if they want to have coffee or go out for lunch. This might be a coworker you seldom connect with or someone who has few friends. Intentionally connect with someone who is different. Who might that be?

  She is the liberal if I am conservative, and rich if I am poor. He is the guy who does not go to the same places I go, the family that does not worship where I worship or shop where I shop. The other is the person from the neighborhood I avoid; the guy I don't want sitting next to me on the plane.

  If you feel uncomfortable stretching this much, then back off a bit and connect in small ways with someone you have never met.

- Listen to people. Become aware of the people around you and become a great listener.

- Be a "preparer." Preparing involves doing small things that show you care for other people.

You prepare for others when you plan a quiet time with your child, when you set candles on the dinner table, when you shovel your sidewalk, or trim the tree away from the street sign. These are ways of preparing to receive others—in other words, through these activities you prepare a table for others. When we are preparing a table, we are also preparing ourselves.

My wife is great at this. When people come to our home, she does little things (candles, special appetizers, nice table settings) that communicate "You are welcome here." She never has to say it; her preparation speaks loud and clear.

- Pay attention to the people you love: "You can put down the phone and listen to your coworker talk for a minute. You can shut off the radio and play checkers with your child. . . . How much do people matter? How important is it to make room for others?"

- Welcome others into your "group." Quite often we spend time in cliques, our usual group of friends at work or in our personal life. And there are others who would like to spend time with you and your friends but feel uninvited. This week invite them!

four

Learning to Live without Anger

I was supposed to speak at a church retreat in three hours. My plane was a little delayed getting into the Burbank airport, but I felt sure I had plenty of time to get to the retreat site, unpack my bags and rest a little before it was time to speak that evening. My brother, who lives in California, was kind enough to meet me at the airport. We got onto the freeway, and for the first ten minutes we moved along nicely. Then, without any warning, we came to a standstill. Traffic on the 405 was barely moving.

I was so happy to see my brother (it had been almost a year) that I continued to talk and laugh with him, telling stories and catching up on life. After fifteen minutes passed the traffic jam was becoming a concern. My brother continued to talk as normal, showing no signs of irritation. "Boy, this traffic is slow. Do you think it will get better?" I asked. "Yeah, it usually does," he said. Another fifteen minutes passed, and I was no longer irritated, I was closer to irate.

I tried to breathe and relax, but my anger had taken over. I looked at my watch and thought about how long it had taken us to go five miles, and then estimated that we still had forty more to go, and I began thinking, *Thanks to this stupid traffic I am not going to get to the retreat in time to unpack and relax a bit, which means I am probably going to be frazzled and won't do well speaking tonight. Or worse, I may not make it at all—how awful would that be? They flew me all the way out here and I am a "no show"—all because of this traffic! Stupid airplanes! Stupid cars!* All of this was going on inside of me, and it was building. I could feel anger moving through my body.

Then my brother looked at me and noticed the look on my face. It is hard to hide anger. He said, "What's the matter?" I said, "Mike, I am getting really ticked off at this traffic, I mean, we are going to be late at best, and maybe worse." Mike started to smile. "Relax, pal, we're fine." "Fine? We are not fine!" I shot back. "Yes we are. Remember, you are in my world now. I drive this way all of the time. It's always jammed here at this time of day. It opens up in about a mile. We should get there with an hour and half before you need to be there."

My blood pressure lowered slightly. Sure enough, within a few minutes we started moving faster, and soon we were flying along the freeway. He was wrong, though, about his estimated arrival time. We arrived an hour and forty-five minutes ahead of time. I was able to take a shower, rest, pray and relax, and I was ready and refreshed for my talk that evening. Lying in bed that night, I was embarrassed about how angry I had gotten over nothing, but more than that, I wanted to know why and how I got so angry.

For the past few months I had been studying anger—its causes and effects—so it was on my mind and was something I had been praying about for a while. My experience on the 405 made everything clear. In fact, it was a perfect case study on anger. I examined what had happened: I did not expect to hit traffic; my brother did. I began to have fearful thoughts about the consequences of being late; my brother did not. Bottom line: *I got very angry; my brother did not.* Though we had the same outer experience, we reacted differently.

Over the next few months I learned much about anger and how living in the kingdom of God can help us manage it.

UNMET EXPECTATIONS PLUS FEAR

There are different kinds of anger. A common type is visceral anger, the kind that hits us immediately, as when a waiter accidentally spills food onto our lap. There is very little lag time between the action and the reaction. It all happens very fast and our bodies react. We can work on this kind of anger, but it is not something we can prepare for. Jesus' apprentices can learn to respond differently to *visceral anger*, but this will take time.

A second type of anger, one that is more common and more damaging to the soul, is *meditative anger*. This kind of anger grows over a period of time. The more we stew on it, the worse it becomes. We can work on this anger more easily because we have more time to process the narratives that cause it.

Visceral and meditative anger are fueled by two ingredients, *unmet expectations* and *fear*, that, when united, ignite into a strong emotion. Unmet expectations are the occasion for anger. For example, we agree to meet a friend for lunch at noon, but the friend shows up at 12:20. We expected our friend to be there by noon. Most of us would feel a series of emotions, such as mild irritation or worry. But at this point *anger* has not occurred; this situation would not normally send someone into a rage. Most of us sit patiently and wait, and when our friend arrives we ask for an explanation.

But now we add fear. While we wait, we begin to think about why our friend is late. Being late without a good reason shows a lack of respect. So we begin to think this lunch partner is showing us very little respect. *I bet she wouldn't be late if she were dining with the president*, you mutter inwardly. Suddenly anger begins to stir. What does this have to do with fear? We fear we are not valuable, that we are not important. It is good, old-fashioned insecurity. The initial unmet expectation has moved to a level of threat. This person is disrespecting us, disregarding our time and feelings. *How dare she?* The anger builds.

Let's add another unmet expectation: We look at our watch and realize that even if our partner arrives in the next second, our lunch time has been reduced. We will have to order hurriedly, eat hastily and perhaps be a few minutes late to the next appointment. Our expectation of a nice, leisurely lunch with good food and conversation has now been destroyed. We cycle back to the thoughts of disrespect, and the anger builds. *Not only does she not care about making me wait, she also has no regard for my well-being.* At this point we are seething.

Then let's say our friend arrives and tells us cavalierly that she almost forgot about lunch, and by the way, "Sorry for being a little late." Now our fears are legitimized: this person *forgot* us, therefore, we are not important. In this case, the tardy person will likely feel the heat of anger. Perhaps we will attack her verbally: "How could you forget! Am I that unimportant to you? I can't believe you made me wait here for twenty minutes—and not even call!" Or perhaps we will be passive-aggressive, growing quiet and barely speaking. Or more commonly, perhaps we will make a snide comment: "That's typical of you, isn't it?" Any way, we want our friend to feel our anger. We cannot let her off the hook.

But let's play it out another way. Our friend arrives late with a gash on her head and explains that she was in a fender-bender and had to deal with the other driver and the police for the last twenty minutes. "I actually would have been here early for lunch. I am so sorry about making you wait." What happens to our anger? It disappears. Instantly. And now a new set of emotions emerge: shame for being angry, sorrow for her condition and concern for her well-being. We go from anger to compassion in a matter of seconds.

Note that everything that has transpired has occurred internally. The unmet expectation was mildly annoying, as they always are. Traffic jams, slow bank tellers and long lines at the grocery store usually make us irritated. But there is no perceived threat at this point. No one is directly hurting us. In fact, no one is to blame. It is only when we are threatened in some way that we get angry. Where does the "threat" come from?

Life is full of unmet expectations. Each day, I estimate, we encounter anywhere from ten to one hundred of them, and we cannot control them. But we can control, or at least better manage, our fears by living in the kingdom of God. We first need to examine the narratives that lead to anger, and then dig a little deeper to find out where they come from. Once we have done this, we can replace the false narratives with the narratives of Jesus.

FALSE IMPERATIVE NARRATIVES (FINS)

Throughout this series we have looked at false narratives that cause so many of our problems (such as believing that God will punish us for our sins). When it comes to anger, the narratives behind this emotion have a unique, imperative quality to them. *Imperative* implies command and control and usually is expressed using words like *must*,

> Which of the FINs are you familiar with?

always and *never.* The following are a list of "imperative narratives" that I believe are the causes of anger, frustration and stress.

- I am alone.
- Things always have to go as I want them.
- Something terrible will happen if I make a mistake.
- I must be in control all of the time.
- Life must always be fair and just.
- I need to anticipate everything that will happen to me today.
- I need to be perfect all of the time.

Each narrative is full of fear and the need to be in control. Our problem is fear, and we think control is the solution.

Take, for example, "I must be in control all of the time." The fear behind this narrative is that if I am not in control, things will go very badly. The narrative expands to include the many ways the world will fall apart when we are not in charge. If we cannot control our work environment, things will go badly and we will lose our job and become poor and not be able to eat. If we cannot control the economy, the weather or our family members, then all hell will break loose. This need to control leads us to turn to our own resources, which is an occasion for sin—"walking in the flesh."

WALKING IN THE FLESH

Paul uses the phrase *walking in the flesh* in opposition to *being led by the Spirit.* "Live by the Spirit, I say, and do not gratify the desires of the flesh. For what the flesh desires is opposed to the Spirit, and what the Spirit desires is opposed to the flesh" (Galatians 5:16-17).

Many people assume that *flesh* refers to the body. But the "flesh" here is not the physical body but rather living from one's own resources, in opposition to (or at least neglect of) God and his resources. The early church preacher John Chrysostom wrote, "The flesh is not the body, nor the essence of the body, but an evil disposition." There is a disposition within us that is prone to wander from God, and when we roam we are "walking in the flesh." Those who live (or walk) in the flesh rely on their own capacity to solve problems.

When people think of fleshly or carnal sins, they think of lust and fornication, or drunkenness and carousing, which certainly are carnal. These behaviors are used to find happiness in something other than God. But fleshly sins also include pride and jealousy, worry and false judgment, resentment and anger. Unrighteous anger rarely happens when we are led by the Spirit. It is spawned by not seeing our situation in light of God's kingdom.

Explain how living in the flesh is sinful.

JESUS' NARRATIVE

The very first issue of the heart Jesus addresses in the Sermon on the Mount is anger.

> You have heard that it was said to those of ancient times, "You shall not murder"; and "whoever murders shall be liable to judgment." But I say to you that if you are angry with a brother or sister, you will be liable to judgment; and if you insult a brother or sister, you will be liable to the council; and if you say, "You fool," you will be liable to the hell of fire. (Matthew 5:21-22)

Many people believe that righteousness is determined by external actions, and therefore if we have not outwardly broken a commandment (e.g., struck or killed someone) we have kept the law and are therefore considered righteous. But Jesus goes deeper, into the heart, the place where all actions spring. He says, "if you are angry with a brother or sister, you will be liable to judgment."

Why? Is he making it harder to be righteous? Is he raising the bar so that no one can make it? Is he more strict than Moses? No. Jesus understands the human heart—and the heart is his primary concern, not merely outward actions. The heart full of anger, the heart that hates, is not far from the heart that *would* murder. In fact, it is essentially the same inner condition. All that is missing is the actual act. Jesus understands that an angry person *would* actually harm someone if he or she *could* get away with it.

When Jesus commands his apprentices not to be angry, he is showing us the way to a good and beautiful life. His command implies that we can actually do it. Many people cannot imagine living without anger. But it is possible, otherwise Jesus would not have instructed us to live without it. Unfortunately, if we hear the command "do not be angry" and think we must do this on our own strength (i.e., in the flesh), we will fail and will begin to resent Jesus for commanding it. For an explanation of how we learn to live without anger, we have to look at the rest of Jesus' teachings, his overall narratives.

The narratives of the kingdom of God are quite different from the FINs. Here they are side by side:

False Imperative Narratives	Kingdom Narratives
I am alone.	You are never alone. Jesus is with you always.
I must be in control all of the time.	Jesus is in control.
Something terrible will happen if I make a mistake.	Mistakes happen all of the time, and things usually work out fine.
Life must always be fair and just.	Life is not always fair and just, but God gets the last word.
I need to be perfect all of the time.	Jesus accepts me—even though I am not perfect.

These kingdom narratives are based on the reality of the presence and power of God. For Jesus, the kingdom was not simply a nice idea, but a very real place—life with God, which is available to all. Outside the kingdom of God we are on our own. We must protect ourselves, fight for our rights and punish those who offend us. Inside the kingdom of God, life is much different. God is with us, protecting us and fighting for our well-being. Knowing this, much of our anger will diminish.

Where do you think perfection comes from?

From fear to trust. In the kingdom of God, Jesus informs us, we can trust our heavenly Father. I learned about trust a few years ago. My daughter Hope and I were at one of my son's many baseball games. She went off to a swing with a friend. She never left my field of vision, but I moved from one part of the stands to another. When she turned to see me in the stands she thought that I was gone; she welled up with tears and began running to the stands. Only about thirty seconds went by, but within that time she lost her breath and began panting with fear. I said, "Hope, I am over here," and she came running. "How could you leave me!" she said, trembling. "I never left you," I said, "and I never lost sight of you. You just lost sight of me." She calmed down quickly, but the fear took a while to subside.

We may lose sight of God, but God never loses sight of us. God gives us space to experiment, grow and mature; God never intrudes. But this doesn't mean God is not with us, is not watching us, is not intimately familiar with our comings and goings. Jesus promised: "I will never leave you or forsake you." Jesus' narrative is that God permits nothing to happen to us that he cannot redeem and use for good. In the kingdom of heaven God is always near. We are never alone and never need to be afraid. When I live with

How does trust diffuse anger?

this reality deep in my mind and heart, anger cannot get a grip on me. I certainly have many unmet expectations each day, but when fear is not present, anger does not arise.

To make headway with our anger, we need to fill our minds with kingdom narratives. Andrew Lester writes,

> How do people change? . . . [C]hange occurs only when a person's stories are reconfigured, reframed, or re-authored. . . . The only way to change is to change our narrative. . . . We have the capacity to develop new images—that is, new narratives—to replace those that produce undesirable "scripts" (stories) which make us vulnerable to anger.

We *can* change our narratives. It will not be quick or easy, but it is possible.

THE CASE FOR ANGER

Before discussing how to deal with anger in healthy ways, it is important to recognize what is good about anger. God designed us with the

capacity for anger. Yet all of us are embarrassed by our angry out-
bursts, which often leave a trail of hurt and pain. So, why did God
make anger possible? Anger is the correct response to injustice, and
we are naturally opposed to injustice because we are created in the
image of a just God. Many Christians think anger is always sinful and
therefore repress or swallow it, which is not the best way to deal with
anger. Becoming angry, in some cases, is the right course of action.

There are two instances in the Gospels when Jesus got angry. The
first was when the Pharisees missed the point of the law (in this case,
when Jesus healed on the sabbath [Mk 3:5]). The other is when Jesus
drove the money changers out of the temple:

> Then Jesus entered the temple and drove out all who were selling
> and buying in the temple, and he overturned the tables of the
> money changers and the seats of those who sold doves. He said
> to them, "It is written, 'My house shall be called a house of prayer';
> but you are making it a den of robbers." (Matthew 21:12-13)

Jesus was clearly angry, yet he was also sinless. Therefore, being
angry is not *always* sinful. In fact, Jesus' anger was completely justified. There is such a thing as righteous anger, and there is a right
response to it. "Righteous anger consists in getting angry at the
things that anger God, and then seeking a proper remedy to correct
the wrong."

We ought to be angry about things like child abuse, the rich ex-
ploiting the poor, fraud, deception and neglect. It is right to become
upset about injustice. This
motivates us to work toward
change. In *The Good and Beautiful God* I wrote about the
wrath of God, which is a right
reaction to sin and evil. I used Mothers Against Drunk Driving as an
example of how anger can be constructive and lead to positive
change.

_____

Describe a time when you felt
your anger was righteous.

_____

The apostle Paul counsels, "Be angry but do not sin; do not let the sun go down on your anger, and do not make room for the devil" (Ephesians 4:26-27). By saying "be angry" Paul is not encouraging anger. He recognizes it is a part of life, and instead of repressing it he instructs that we should not let the sun go down on our anger. Archibald Hart explains, "Paul is saying here that it is not the anger itself (the feeling) that is wrong, but that anger has the potential for leading you into sin. To feel anger, to tell someone that you feel angry, and to talk about your anger are both healthy and necessary."

When we let the sun go down on our anger, we allow it to poison our souls. This is why Paul follows with the warning "do not make room for the devil." The Greek word for "room" is *topos*, which means "place or footing." Unexpressed and unresolved anger give the enemy a foothold to work from. Anger easily can be turned into resentment (*Why does she always neglect me?* or *He always gets what I deserve*) and despair (*Life is unfair, why even try?*). So we need to examine the cause of our anger. Perhaps it is righteous anger, which can lead us to correct an injustice. The vast majority of my anger is unrighteous and is a natural outgrowth of the FINs I have to fight.

REMEMBER: CHANGE TAKES TIME

The day I sat in traffic on the 405 freeway was the first day I really examined my anger and began to work toward change, thanks to the prompting and power of the Holy Spirit. Since that day I have come a long way. I understand a lot more about what causes anger and how to diffuse it. But I am not entirely free of anger. Tonight I got mad at my dog because he stole my sandwich. I called him unpleasant things in a not-so-polite tone. But a few minutes later I laughed. I think being able to laugh at ourselves is a

When has God used a trial to shape your character?

pretty good sign that we are progressing. Just remember to give yourself grace. Change is slow. As long as we continue to work on changing our narrative and engage in spiritual exercises, we will see changes.

keeping the sabbath

Keeping the sabbath is a spiritual exercise that can help us better deal with our anger. This may seem strange because anger and sabbath keeping do not seem to have much in common. But there is a strong connection. Anger is about unmet expectations and fear. Sabbath is about trusting God and his ways. As Norman Wirzba notes,

> Sabbath rest is thus a call to Sabbath trust, a call to visibly demonstrate in our daily living that we know ourselves to be upheld and maintained by the grace of God rather than the strength and craftiness of our own hands. To enjoy a Sabbath day, we must give up our desire for total control. We must learn to live by the generosity of manna falling all around us.

Anger is a result of our need to control (unmet expectations) and fear, and the sabbath teaches us to trust in God's strength. Sabbath keeping, therefore, is the perfect exercise to help us deal with anger.

Sabbath forces us out of the role of God in our lives. Allowing God to take care of us, we relax and enjoy life. That is essentially what it means to rest. That is why sleep is such an important part of the sabbath. Sleep is an act of trust. We let go. We trust that no one will harm us even though we have no proof that all will be well.

Rest. Trust. Surrendering control. These are the core elements of sabbath keeping, and they help us deal with anger. But there is even more to sabbath keeping than simply refraining from activity. Sab-

bath keeping is also a matter of joy and delight. Jesus did not keep
the sabbath legalistically. On many occasions he performed actions
on the sabbath that the Pharisees thought were sinful. For example,
he healed people, and on one occasion he and his disciples picked
some corn that they later ate. Jesus smartly observed, "The sabbath
was made for humankind, and not humankind for the sabbath; so
the Son of Man is lord even of the sabbath" (Mark 2:27-28)

Like any other spiritual practice, the sabbath easily degenerates
into legalism. But Jesus says the sabbath is a gift, not a set of laws.
Jesus certainly kept the sabbath, for he never sinned. He kept the sabbath in the right spirit.

How can we practice sabbath keeping? A rule of thumb is to start
small. Here are some of the things I like to do.

- Take some time to plan your sabbath. Which day will you do it?
  What will you do? What will you eat?

- Start in the evening with a special meal for you, your family and
  friends.

- Light a candle or two at the center of the table when everyone has
  come to the table. You might want to use this ancient Jewish
  prayer, typically said by the woman of the home: "Blessed art thou,
  O Lord our God, King of the Universe, who hast sanctified us by
  Thy commandments and commanded us to kindle the Sabbath
  lights."

- During the meal it is customary for the man of the house (the father, if there are children) to bless everyone at the table. I usually
  keep this informal (e.g., I tell my children how much I love them
  and how proud I am of them). This can be very special.

- Play games!

- Eat great food that you love. I live by the unwritten (and unsub-
  stantiated) rule that calories do not count on the sabbath!

- Go to church together (if you choose Sunday as your sabbath).

- Try not to eat out (it makes others work), which will mean having food prepared by you for the next day.

- Nap!

- Set aside some time for private prayer.

- Read a good devotional book or write in your journal.

- Look over the list of blessings you created earlier in the curriculum (in the first book, *The Good and Beautiful God,* pp. 70-71), and give thanks.

- Spend some time reading the Bible—just don't make it a heavy study.

- Practice hospitality—invite friends to eat with you.

A common question: Is there a certain day of the week we should keep the sabbath? In my view, no. For Jewish people and Seventh-day Adventists, it is Saturday (or sundown Friday evening to sundown Saturday evening). But since the fourth century most Christians observed the sabbath on Sunday, the day the Lord rose from the grave. This allowed Christians to honor the ancient sabbath and Jesus' resurrection. Sunday works best for most Christians because they have the day off. Nevertheless, I do not believe that any certain day is the right day. (For pastors, Sunday is about the last day for them to experience rest!)

five

LEARNING TO LIVE
WITHOUT LUST

The phone rang in my office at 3:30 in the afternoon.

"Hey, Dad, this is Jacob." Jacob has seldom called me at work, usually only to ask a favor or pass on information.

"Hey, pal, what's up?

"I just have a question."

"Go ahead," I said.

"When is it OK to kiss a girl?"

I was stunned. He was twelve years old, and I knew this discussion was coming one day, but I was still taken back, especially by his directness. I did not want to make any assumptions, so I asked, "Are you asking because you are thinking about kissing a girl?"

"Um . . . yeah."

"How long have you known her?"

"A while."

"Are you going steady with her?"

"Dad, nobody uses that phrase anymore."

"OK, is she your girlfriend?"

"Kind of."

"This is going to be kind of strange, pal, but can you get out a piece of paper?"

"Sure," he said. I heard the paper rustling in the background.

"Now, I want you to draw a triangle, and then I am going to answer your question," I said.

Over the next twenty minutes I explained the relationship between physical intimacy and relational commitment. Then Jacob said, "I think I get it, Dad. That makes a lot of sense. Thanks."

For at least one day I felt like I had parented well.

A SILENT CHURCH IN A SEX-OBSESSED CULTURE

Contemporary society is obsessed with sexuality and lust. Our magazines are dripping with it; our television programs are obsessed with it; much of our music is nothing short of a series of odes to lust covered in the veneer of love. We are fascinated with sexuality. People live for sex, kill for sex and die because of sex. Over fourteen thousand sexual references are made on TV per year; the average person will view over one hundred thousand of those references in his or her lifetime. An actress on a popular crime drama was asked why her character wore such low cut, revealing outfits (forensics experts usually wear smocks). She answered, "The more cleavage the higher the ratings." We have become so desensitized to sexual imagery that advertisers know that they must use provocative images just to get our attention.

Christians (as well as Muslims, Jews and even nonreligious yet morally concerned people) have tried to stand against the culture and maintain the position that sexual purity, chastity, and fidelity are important. We can go to church, pray, sing hymns and set our minds on things above, and then go home, watch a football game on TV, and be exposed to dozens of commercials and ads for upcoming shows that are full of sex and violence.

My son had seen all those images, heard a lot of misinformation from school friends and was caught in the bewilderment of his own natural desire. Who will help these young people? In fact, who will help us older folk who must find a way to live faithfully in this sexually confused culture. There are two dominant narratives my son had heard—one from the church, the other from popular culture. Both are false, and both lead to frustration and failure. Dallas Willard notes, "The two main errors in the area of human sexuality are these: (1) assuming that all sexual desire is good, and (2) believing that all sexual desire is evil."

THE FALSE CHRISTIAN NARRATIVE:
ALL SEXUAL DESIRE IS EVIL

The first narrative says that sexual desire is inherently sinful. It has been dominant in Christian circles from the beginning of church history. There are many early Christian writers to whom we can trace this belief, but perhaps the most famous is the brilliant and influential writer Augustine of Hippo. Augustine, writing in the fourth and fifth centuries, was of the opinion that sexual desire was sinful. He even said that sexual intercourse transmits original sin and is essentially sinful.

Augustine wrestled with lust throughout his life, which is clear when you read his *Confessions*. Augustine prayed, "Lord, make me chaste, . . . but not yet," which is a clear indication of inner conflict. He eventually adopted the narrative that sexual desire is bad; complete celibacy is good. Augustine's writings have dominated the thinking of most Christians—Catholics and Protestants—for the past fifteen hundred years. But he was not the only person who adopted this narrative.

Throughout the history of the church—before and after Augustine—few Christian thinkers espouse a positive position on human sexual desire. The vast majority speak of sexuality as dark, evil and sinful. Up to the medieval period, some of the most spiritually dedi-

cated men and women lived in monasteries, where they would rarely
see someone of the opposite sex, lest they be tempted to sin. Even in
our day many churches have difficulty articulating a balanced view
of human sexuality.

The church's narrative is not broadcast but comes through relative
silence: don't ask, don't tell, don't talk about sex. Of course, youth
pastors occasionally address the subject, but with fear and trembling,
parental permission, and a measure of embarrassment. But it is rarely
addressed from the pulpit or in Sunday school. The subject is taboo.
Yet those sitting in the pews are having affairs, struggling with pornography and wrestling with lust as Augustine did.

Which of these false
narratives were you
most exposed to
growing up? How did
this affect your life?

By refusing to address sexuality, we
imply it is sinful. Our silence causes
confusion, leads to ignorance and further separates our souls from our bodies. When we hear about the sexual failings of our pastors and priests, we are
doubly shocked: *How could a holy person do such a thing?* we wonder in an-
guish. Christians, it appears, come up from the waters of baptism
having been made "eunuchs for the kingdom." Our silent narrative
leads to shame and denial about something that ought to be
affirmed.

THE FALSE WORLDLY NARRATIVE:
ALL SEXUAL DESIRE IS GOOD

The second false narrative comes from contemporary Western culture: "All sexual desire is good." This narrative is not a product of
the twentieth or twenty-first centuries. The sexual attitudes and
behaviors of the Roman emperor Caligula or some of the Greek
philosophers would make us blush. It may be more pervasive today
though.

The narrative that all sexual desire is good became accepted in

American culture in the 1960s as young people espoused free love. Hugh Hefner created the "Playboy Philosophy," which taught that sex is a purely natural act and that everyone ought to have as much as they want. Today we see it most clearly in television and movies, where the majority of sexual activity occurs outside of marriage. In music videos barely clothed women dance provocatively and the lyrics are lusty compositions about the joys of sex. The implicit narrative is that the good life is the lust-filled, sexually libertine life.

About the only restriction on sexual behavior today is that we must never harm or take advantage of another person. Sexual activity must always be consensual. Beyond this, the dominant narrative is, "If people want something, it is acceptable." This has opened our culture to practices that historically have been rejected. Things that formerly shocked us now barely register a response. In an age of tolerance we have simply become desensitized.

A MEASURE OF TRUTH

How did these narratives become so prevalent? Both contain a measure of truth, as do all of the false narratives. Yes, sexual desire does lead people to behaviors they later regret. It is behind extramarital affairs, promiscuity and Internet pornography, but it is wrong to blame the desire itself. We don't say the desire for food is evil because it leads some people to gluttony, or that thirst is evil because it leads some people to drunkenness.

Our culture's narrative also contains some truth: sexual desire is indeed good. God's first command to Adam and Eve was to "be fruitful and multiply," which concerned sexuality. It was designed by God; it is how we perpetuate the species and is a great enhancement to marriage. But simply because it is commanded by God does not mean there are no boundaries; simply because it is natural does not mean it is always right; simply because it feels good does not mean it is always good. Not all sexual desires and expressions are good, and not all are bad.

JESUS' NARRATIVE: *EPITHUMIA* IS THE PROBLEM

Jesus knew how important sexuality is, how it can destroy life or enhance life. He spoke to the issue in Sermon on the Mount. Unfortunately, it is often misunderstood, which contributes to our problem with sexuality.

> You have heard that it was said, "You shall not commit adultery." But I say to you that everyone who looks at a woman with lust has already committed adultery with her in his heart. If your right eye causes you to sin, tear it out and throw it away; it is better for you to lose one of your members than for your whole body to be thrown into hell. And if your right hand causes you to sin, cut it off and throw it away; it is better for you to lose one of your members than for your whole body to go into hell. (Matthew 5:27-30)

This passage has led many to believe Jesus is saying that simply looking at a woman lustfully is the *same* as committing adultery. It certainly appears that way. But a closer look reveals something different.

The word that is used for lust in this passage is *epithumia*. This word had a very specific meaning. It does not refer to ordinary sexual attraction but to *intentionally objectifying another person for one's own gratification*. When I discuss this issue with students, I describe it this way: *Epithumia* is not referring to the first look but to the *second*. The first look may be simple attraction, but the second look is leering. Lust does not value the person but mere body parts.

Explain how a lustful person has the same inner condition as an adulterer?

Epithumia goes beyond mere sexual attraction. It intentionally cultivates sexual desire for the sake of the feeling itself. It is the opposite of love. Love looks into the eyes; *epithumia* steals glances below them. Love values the other as a person; *epithumia* degrades the other. We must make a clear distinction between attraction and objectification, between feeling sexual desire and *epithumia*. When we fail to make the distinction, we adopt the first false narrative and think that sexual attraction is evil in itself.

One day I was walking on the beach with my brother, engaged in a deep conversation about God. A beautiful young woman in a bikini was walking in our direction, and of course we both noticed her. When she passed by we looked at each other and said, "Wow." Now, had we sinned at that point? I don't think so. If we had not noticed, we would not be sexual persons. The response was completely acceptable in my view. Now, had we turned and followed her, focusing our eyes on her body, dreaming of a sexual encounter with her, we would have sinned. We would have crossed over from simple sexual attraction to *epithumia*. But we didn't.

A NEW KIND OF PERSON

Jesus is teaching about the difference between *inner* and *outer* righteousness, and on becoming a new kind of person in the kingdom of God. Jesus is most concerned with the heart, particularly with developing a good heart. A good heart is free from objectification for the sake of self-gratification. In the kingdom of God we are being transformed into a new kind of person, based on our new identity as "one indwelt by Christ." Such persons will develop inner character that is not dominated by sexual desire.

In Jesus' day adultery was defined as sexual contact between persons, at least one of whom is married, who are not married to each other. The difference between our day and Jesus' day is that adultery was applied almost exclusively to women. A man, even a married man, could have sex with other women, including slaves and prostitutes. But a woman was allowed to have sex with her husband alone. The charge of adultery usually resulted in the execution of the accused woman. But in Matthew 5:27-30 Jesus is speaking directly to men.

Jesus explains to men that *epithumia* is a form of adultery. In adultery sexual desire triumphs over a person's commitments. Adultery implies, "Fulfilling my desire is more important than fulfilling my commitment. I don't care if I hurt others; right now all I care about is me." The same is true of lust: valuing the other as a sacred being is tossed aside. Jesus brilliantly gets to the heart of the matter. He invites us into the kingdom in order to become new people—people who value and respect others.

EPITHUMIA FOR WOMEN

Some women have told me that they think *epithumia* is strictly a male problem: "I don't objectify men's body parts; I don't look at men to cultivate lustful feelings." But I believe that while there are women who do not lust the same *way*, they still wrestle with *epithumia*. It just gets expressed differently. (Please note that what I am about to say is not true of all women, just as it is not true of all men.)

Epithumia usually involves objectifying a *body*. But it can also involve objectifying a *persona*. While some women do not struggle with objectifying male bodies, they do struggle with objectifying a man's persona. Take, for example, romance novels or chick flicks. A lonely and misunderstood woman is rescued by a man ("Dirk" or "Brock") who whisks her away on his white horse (think Cinderella and you have the plot of 90 percent of romance novels). The man whispers into her ear that she is the woman of his dreams and he will love, care for and protect her forever.

Women are fulfilling emotional needs—to feel loved and valued, to feel special and sacred—through romance novels. Dirk provides that feeling. But Dirk is not real. And therein lays the problem. He is a fantasy. He is an object worth a second, third and fourth look. There is no interaction, no intimacy, no relationship, no mutual enhancement. The reader is simply fantasizing because it feels good.

I once remarked to a class of graduate students that I thought romance novels were a female version of porn. Most of the women were shocked at the comparison. But a few months later an older, single woman said to me, "When you compared romance novels to porn I was really offended because I read a lot of those novels. But I started to think about what you said, about objectifying the persona, which is really *epithumia*, and I realized you are right. I have a secret stash of my favorite romance novels, and they are all dog-eared at the juiciest parts so I could take a second look." Dirk is really no different than the centerfold; it's just that one is mental and other is visual.

If you are a woman who does not read romance novels or watch a lot of chick flicks, you may be thinking, *Once again, this does not relate to me.* But have you ever thought about how so-and-so has "the perfect husband" or "the ideal boyfriend"? Do you ever fantasize about the man of your dreams? This can be a form of *epithumia*.

Finally, many women struggle with Internet pornography. And some women are deeply troubled by how much they think about and desire sex. The point is that both men and women struggle with *epithumia*. The good news is that the solution to the problem is for both men and women.

> Though the expressions may vary, what is the central issue both men and women share in the struggle with *epithumia*?

LIVING IN THE KINGDOM IS THE CURE FOR *EPITHUMIA*

In the kingdom of God we learn a new set of stories. As we live in the kingdom we learn that God is good, and we learn to see everything through God's eyes. Living in the kingdom, and thereby changing our false narratives to kingdom narratives, is the solution to overcoming *epithumia*. Too many people repeatedly try—and fail—to deal with lust through their willpower and tearful prayers but find no genuine change. We cannot change our heart by changing outer behavior alone. This is why Jesus spoke about plucking out our eye when it offends us.

Jesus was not speaking literally but was using a rhetorical device

called reductio ad absurdum, meaning to reduce the argument to its
logical absurdity. He was attacking the commonly held notion that
sin resides in the offending part of the body. This is why some cul-
tures cut off the hand of a thief. They reason: cut off the sinful part,
and the sin will be gone. "If your right eye causes you to sin," Jesus
says, "tear it out."

As Dallas Willard often jokes, "Jesus is not here advocating that
we cut off every offending part so we can roll into heaven as a bloody
stump!" He is taking their logic to that absurd conclusion. The problem is not in our hand or our eye—the lust is in our heart. To be sure,
our body is involved in the act, but the real culprit is inward, in the
imagination, in the heart. I lust—or cultivate lust (epithumia)—when
I feel empty and have nowhere to put my strong desires. When I am
not in close union with God and his kingdom, I have a void in my
soul. I want to feel something, to be caught up in something, and
when I am disconnected from God and his kingdom, one of the most
thrilling alternatives is epithumia.

Epithumia allows me to feel a very strong and good sensation. But
like the Turkish Delight candy in The Lion, the Witch, and the Wardrobe, it does not satisfy but leaves us wanting more. The desire is so
strong that we are prepared to do anything to have it. How does living in the kingdom of God help? When we are properly connected to
God and his kingdom we find that the void is filled.

> How might living
> closely with God in
> his kingdom help you
> deal with *epithumia*?

Living in the kingdom is like an adventure. I never know how and when God
is going to work in my life, but God always seems to do something at the right
time, in the right way. Not long ago I was
working on a ministry project that was on
the edge of failure. At precisely the right moment a new opportunity and
new resources were made available. All I could do was smile. Working
with God and his kingdom has been like that for me over and over.

In the kingdom we know who we are and whose we are. The need to feel loved, to be important, and to be sacred and special is met in our oneness with Christ. When I set my heart on things above (the kingdom) I discover that I am part of something thrilling and exciting—the divine conspiracy—and everywhere I turn God is at work. Now I have the drama I seek, and I have a place to channel my energies. Rob Bell observes,

> If it's just me against the lust, the odds are always against me. . . . Whatever it is that has its hooks in you, you will never be free until you find something you want more. It's not about getting rid of desire. It's about giving ourselves to bigger and better and more powerful desires. . . . Life is not about toning down and repressing your God-given life force. It's about channeling it and focusing it and turning it loose on something beautiful.

Finally, because I know who I am and am secure (God is good and desires my good) I am free to see others in a new way. I no longer see them as objects to exploit but as real persons who God dearly loves.

Joy. Gratitude. Thanksgiving. Grace. These are kingdom words. When we live with God in his kingdom, we begin to love our life. Rob Bell says this is essential when dealing with *epithumia*: "Gratitude is so central to the life God made us for. Until we can center ourselves on what we do have, on what God has given us, on the life we do get to live, we'll constantly be looking for another life." Lust is really about spiritual hunger for God and his kingdom. Therefore our sexual problems are resolved when we enroll as Jesus' apprentices in his glorious kingdom.

THE LEVEL OF APPROPRIATE PHYSICAL INTIMACY

When I was in college, professor Richard Foster used a triangle diagram to answer essentially the same question my son had: What is the appropriate level of physical intimacy? Or how far is too far? The diagram helped me a great deal, and I hoped it would help my son. Imagine a triangle with one angle at the top. The two sides rising from the base represent two aspects of a relationship: one, the level of commitment, and the other, the level of physical intimacy. The base of the triangle represents a relationship with no physical intimacy and no commitment.

As the level of commitment rises, so can the level of physical intimacy. The point of the diagram is to illustrate that physical intimacy must be matched by an appropriate level of commitment. On a first or second date, for example, there is very little commitment, so kissing is not appropriate. But as the commitment level rises, the level of intimacy can rise as well because each person has been properly valued.

Think about people who engage in sexual activity without any commitment. They are diminished by it. Ask them later (especially as they are about to marry someone else) about their past, and inevitably they will feel regret, remorse or even shame. Something important transpires between sexually intimate persons. And that is the genius of Richard's triangle: we are sacred beings and should treat one another as such. Where the two sides come together at the top illustrates that the highest act of physical intimacy—sexual intercourse—can only be sustained by the highest level of commitment—marriage.

The triangle illustrates something else that many Christians need to hear. Not all physical intimacy in developing relationships is evil and should be forbidden. I knew a guy in college who said he was not going to kiss his girlfriend until they were married. While the intention may be honorable, in reality it is not healthy. And it can lead to a very negative view of sexuality. A couple shared with me that when they went to Christian camps as teenagers they were told that all physical intimacy was sinful. Each year camp speakers would say they had given up dating and would not touch their spouse-to-be until their wedding night. They were lauded as role models. As a result, the teens were sent a clear message: physical intimacy is taboo.

The couple said very honestly, "When we got engaged and then married, we had a hard time expressing physical intimacy because all we heard for years was the narrative, 'Sex is bad and evil. So save it for marriage!'"

I shared the illustration with my son because I wanted to show him that physical intimacy is a good thing between people who are committed to each other. Nevertheless, the vast majority of sexual failure happens when physical intimacy exceeds commitment. But that does not mean we ought to abandon physical intimacy altogether. Within proper boundaries, it is a God-given gift to be treasured.

I remember performing the wedding of a committed and loving Christian couple. During premarital counseling the woman shared, with her fiancé present, "My fiancé had sexual intercourse with several women in his past. This hurt me because I saved myself for him. But he did that when he was young, and he has changed since he began following Christ. And we have waited until marriage. But I have to tell you that one day while praying about it, I realized that I will have to deal with that fact forever. That is a part of his soul." Her words are very instructive. We are not just dealing with bodies but also with our souls. That is why this is such an important subject.

A few days after our talk I asked my son, "So, did you kiss that girl?" I had been careful not to give him a strict rule, but to allow him to figure it out on his own. Rules are easily rebelled against; wisdom is much better.

"Nah."

"Why not?" I asked.

"The reason I asked you was because some of the kids at school were all saying it was cool just to kiss someone for fun, and one guy teased me because I hadn't kissed a girl yet. But it didn't seem right just to do it. The triangle thing made sense. I am not committed to her, and I don't know her very well."

I was so proud of him. He was so wise for his age. I would like to take some credit, but I think he wouldn't have kissed even if we had not talked. There is one thing I am sure that Jacob knows: Christ dwells in him. I have been telling him that (well, the Holy Spirit has) since he was young. The fact that he said, "it didn't seem right," led me to believe he would have made the right decision, not because of a rule or a law but because he knows who he is. He didn't need the triangle, but now he has it in his mind. When he goes on dates now my wife says to him, "Remember the triangle." We all smile.

ONE FINAL WORD

Over the years I have worked with many people, mostly men, who have struggled with *epithumia*. Their stories are painful and their anguish is very real. They say things like, "I want more than anything to change." And yet, they come back again and again saying, "I still keep failing." Some, however, come back and share that they have seen real change in their life, that they are no longer dominated by sexual desires. What made the difference? Is there any common denominator between those who find freedom and those who don't?

To put it simply: *We must really want to change*. I know this sounds simplistic and even harsh to those who fail. "But I do want to change! How dare you say I don't!" When I have probed deeply into the person's heart, I have discovered that they do not really want to change; they merely dislike the consequences of the failure (the guilt, the embarrassment, the shame). In order to find freedom from lust a person must really be sick of it and understand its nature. Many have said they wanted to change, but in reality they nurse a love of lust. Promises, pledges and resolutions are no match for a heart that secretly cherishes sin and merely dislikes its consequences.

Those who have overcome *epithumia* have exposed it for what it is: a false and short-lived feeling of pleasure that ultimately harms life. We can begin to change only when we see *epithumia* for what it is. Then we need to cultivate something else in its place: a strong sense of our worth, love and appreciation for life in the kingdom, and healthy relationships that bring us the intimacy we long for. Then we find freedom. If you struggle with this, be encouraged. Countless people have overcome it.

Begin by praying for the desire to change. Ask God to instill wisdom to see *epithumia* for what it is. Pray for a strong desire for purity. This powerful prayer is often the first step toward real and lasting change.

SOUL TRAINING

media fast

In this chapter we have discussed how sexually saturated our culture is. This week I am asking you to consider fasting from all media for two days. This will be challenging, but don't be alarmed: so far no one has died from it. The forty-eight-hour media fast includes

- the Internet
- television
- newspapers and magazines
- radio stations
- video games
- iPods, mp3 players and stereos

What will you do with your time? How will you entertain yourself? Try playing a board game or card game with your friends. Read a book. One young woman said, "I probably spend four to five hours a day on MySpace and Facebook, so with all of that free time I ended up reading two books I have been wanting to read. It was great. And I didn't miss a thing by not going on-line for forty-eight hours."

Take a walk, get coffee with friends, exercise. You are beginning to change your mind (*metanoia*), which has been filled with false narratives about who you are and what life is about. For forty-eight hours free your mind from the junk; give some space to the Holy

Spirit to renew your thinking. This is your way of saying, "I am not under the dominion of media. I am going to show that I can live without it."

Though no one has died or been harmed by this exercise, it still may be a challenge. One young man said the temptation to check his Facebook page is the most difficult and painful thing he has faced in his Christian life. But he learned he can do it. He said, "So I figured, if I can say no to that—which was really, really tempting—then I can say no to the temptation of *epithumia*." Brilliant connection! Some people think overcoming lust is impossible, as if it were as strong and compelling as gravity. But it isn't. We choose to engage in *epithumia*, just as we choose to spend four hours in chat rooms or watching movies. We can say no!

SIX

Learning to Live
without Lying

I was at a dinner party with ten couples, all of whom were very well educated. Someone introduced me to a man by saying, "Jim, here, teaches at a college." The other man said, "Oh, an academic type. Great! I love to talk to fellow academics." For the record, I have never thought of myself as an academic type. I just like to study and to teach. Nonetheless, the man started to tell me about a course he was teaching on literature. He said, "I think Hawthorne was the most brilliant writer of his generation, by far. Don't you, Jim?"

"Well, he was quite good," I said, having never read a single sentence of Hawthorne.

"Quite good? The best. Anyway, I was making this point that the genius of *The Scarlet Letter* is in its irony. I mean, the fact that the accusers are the true sinners, and the accused sinner is actually the most righteous character. Do you agree, Jim?"

"Well, uh, . . . yes, yes, I agree."

Again, I had never read Hawthorne, but I now knew something he wrote. The conversation lasted another painful ten minutes, and each time he asked one of his questions I responded with a carefully crafted lie. I began to get nervous, afraid that at any moment he would ask an open-ended question I would be unable to answer. It would be clear I had never read the book, and everyone would know that I was a fraud, a fake, a liar.

So why did I persist? I had so little to gain and so much to lose. Why did I not respond to his very first question by saying, "Actually, as strange as this may seem to you, I have never read Hawthorne"? What kept me from being honest? The question is especially probing because I, like most everyone, think that lying is a sin. And like most people, I do not like being lied to. It feels disrespectful, at the very least. So I don't like being lied to, I think it is a sin, and I know it of-fers little gain at a high risk.

> How would you answer these really tough questions: How often do you lie? Do you consider yourself a liar? Reflect a bit on this practice in your own life.

There must be some narrative that drives this inconsistent behavior. To tell the truth, I lie a fair amount. And so do you, I suspect. We all lie a lot more than we realize because we have a strong and intricate system of rationalization that justifies our deceptions. I want to explore why we lie, what Jesus said about it and how we can begin to cure our need to lie.

LIARS AND CHEATERS

Apparently I am not the only person who lies. See if you have told any of these lies:

- Yes, I have read that book (or seen that movie).

- Yes, let's definitely get together soon.

- He's in a meeting.

- She's not home.

- No, that outfit doesn't make you look fat.

According to a study conducted by Robert Feldman, in a ten-minute conversation we tell an average of 3.3 lies—once every three minutes or so. The most shocking study I have ever seen concluded that we are lied to every five minutes, or an average of two hundred times a day. Author Ralph Keyes, who has written an excellent book on lying, concludes that "some form of deception occurs in nearly two-thirds of all conversations." In another study, 59 percent of two thousand American parents admitted to lying to their children on a regular basis: "Our cable company doesn't get that TV show"; "If you touch that button it could shock you"; "The candy store is closed." And yet, nearly all parents do not want their children to lie and have no tolerance when their children lie to them. Keyes concludes, "If research on this subject is credible, nearly all of us tell lies, and far more often than we realize."

Author David Callahan broadens the category of lying to include cheating, which is a form of lying. Cheating involves deception with the intent to gain something. Consider some of the following examples that Callahan cites:

- Many wealthy parents take their kids "diagnosis shopping." That is, they go to multiple doctors until they find one who will say their child has a slight learning disability because "an official diagnosis of disability will allow their kids more time on the SATs." A better score may get them into a better college.

- Personnel officers estimate that nearly 25 percent of the information they see on résumés is not just "padding" but "gross misinformation."

- As many as two million Americans have illegal offshore bank accounts they use to evade taxes.

- Thousands of Americans are knowingly "pirating" cable TV.

"Americans are now stealing $6 billion a year worth of paid television."

- A 2002 undercover sting operation in New Jersey found 350 examples of fraudulent practices at auto repair centers, "mainly for the performance of unnecessary repairs. Some estimates of the cost nationwide of auto-repair fraud run as high as $40 billion a year." By the way, they only examined *six* auto repair centers.

Callahan concludes, "Americans are not only cheating more in many areas but are also feeling less guilty about it." Something seems to have shifted in the last few decades. And yet, in study after study people still consider truth-telling to be one of the most important of all virtues. People feel violated when they discover they have been lied to. And yet we are a nation of liars. We are in conflict about this matter, "excusing our lies at the same time that we are appalled by the prevalence of dishonesty."

We need to get inside the matter and discover the causes of lying. Once we understand it, we can get at the source of the problem and find ways to change.

FALSE NARRATIVE: I NEED TO LIE TO GET BY

Our behavior is rooted in our narratives. So if we are a nation of liars, there must be a narrative beneath the surface that encourages us or at least permits us to lie. Given that we have a deep need to think well of ourselves, when we lie we need an excuse.

- I don't want to have to deal with someone else's hurt feelings.

- It was just a white lie. I meant no harm.

- If I told the truth, I would get in trouble.

- The ends justify the means.

The essence of all of the excuses is utilitarian. This utilitarian narrative says, "I am important, and my well-being is my main mission. There will be times that I will need to lie in order to gain what I want or prevent something I do not want. That is why lying is OK." It is a means-ends justification. The means (lying) may not in itself be morally right, but the ends (what we gain or what punishment we avoid) justifies the means. Thus the two main things that drive us to lie are: (1) fear of what will happen if we tell the truth, and (2) desire for personal gain if we lie. Let's take a closer look at both of these.

Fear. Most of our lying is fear-based: we lie to avoid trouble. For example, a mother walks into the kitchen and sees her two-year-old covered with flour, and asks, "Billy, did you spill the flour?" The little boy thinks about the consequences of telling the truth, and without missing a beat, says, "No, mamma." Why? Fear. He feared the consequences of telling the truth. Children, by the way, are usually terrible liars. It takes years to perfect the practice, because effective lying involves overriding our bodies. Even then, it is difficult to fool a lie detection machine. Our bodies seem to be opposed to lying.

> Examine a recent lie you told. Was it driven by fear or desire?

When asked a question like "Did you cheat on that exam?" "Did you ever love someone before you met me?" or "Is that your best offer?" we are mindful that our answer will cause us either pain or pleasure, and we vastly prefer pleasure. One time I caught a student plagiarizing. I discovered that his entire paper was lifted from the Internet—every word. I asked him to come to my office. "Are you telling me that this paper is entirely your own work and that you did not use any other sources to help in this paper?" I asked.

"Yes," he said, with defiance in his voice.

I pulled out a copy of the Internet article and handed it to him. He buried his hands in his face. He then confessed that the work was not his own. He had first lied to me by turning in a false paper, and lied again directly to me. One lie led to the next until he realized he was caught. Why did he do this? Fear. He told me he had procrastinated, and at the last minute used the Internet as a shortcut. He believed that if he turned in his own work, he would get a bad grade. He was afraid of getting a failing grade—afraid enough to commit a highly unethical act with great consequences.

Desire. We also lie when we think we might gain something we want. Over the past few years we increasingly hear stories of people who lied on their résumés in order to get a certain job. Desire propels them to lie. People lie about their age, their marital status, their education and their occupation in order to get something they want. They say they don't intend to hurt anyone; they just want to be liked or accepted or get the job. We use a common rationalization that is tied to one of our dominant narratives. We tell ourselves: My needs are more important than anything else.

The false imperative narratives from the chapter on anger also contribute to the need to lie: "It is all about me, and I am alone." The first clause justifies all of our actions; the second clause forces us to use our own resources, which are limited, to get what we want. One of our fleshly resources is deception. We can be sure that we are not operating within the kingdom when we choose to lie. We are running on our own strength. And it can and does often work. People lie on a résumé and get the job. People lie about the sale price and make more money. They are not in sync or in partnership with the kingdom, but they are getting what they want. And that is all they need to justify the actions.

These are two of the main reasons why we lie: we think we need to (1) in order to get what we want, or (2) to avoid something we don't want. And if the universe revolves around us, then the lying is justified. We now have a narrative that allows us to sleep at night. Unfortunately, we are destroying the integrity of our own souls. According to Jesus, even if we gain the whole world but lose our soul, we have truly lost what is most important.

JESUS' NARRATIVE ABOUT LYING
In the next section of the Sermon, Jesus deals with false speech in

verbal communication. Let's look at his teaching on this subject:

> Again, you have heard that it was said to those of ancient times, "You shall not swear falsely, but carry out the vows you have made to the Lord." But I say to you, Do not swear at all, either by heaven, for it is the throne of God, or by the earth, for it is his footstool, or by Jerusalem, for it is the city of the great King. And do not swear by your head, for you cannot make one hair white or black. Let your word be "Yes, Yes" or "No, No"; anything more than this comes from the evil one. (Matthew 5:33-37)

Jesus is dealing with the issue of "swearing," which does not refer to cussing or using profane language, but to making a verbal promise that what is said is true, such as taking an oath. Once again, he creates a distinction between what is considered "righteous" behavior and the kind of behavior expected of those who live in the kingdom of God.

The "old law" simply states that we must not lie under oath. When a person swears to "tell the truth, the whole truth and nothing but the truth," we demand, by law, that they do so. Perjury, the failure to tell the truth under oath, was a punishable offense in Jesus' day, as it is in ours. Telling the truth is necessary in order to find justice, and that is why the courts insist on it. In order for a society to get along we must be able to trust what someone is saying. But we cannot count on people telling the truth on their own—especially if they fear the consequences, or the desire for gain is involved.

Think about the professional baseball players who were accused of taking performance-enhancing drugs. Under oath, some of them denied using steroids, but were caught later. Others pled the Fifth Amendment, so they wouldn't incriminate themselves. That is precisely why we require that people swear under oath to tell the truth. We cannot count on them to be truthful without it. Unfortunately, even under oath some people lie.

In Jesus' day, swearing went beyond the courtroom and into everyday business transactions, and even into daily communication. For example, when selling a cow, the seller would often "swear by God" or "swear upon" his own life that he was telling the truth about the condition of the cow. Today, to establish their credibility some swear what they are saying is true. Jesus' teaching on this is very clear: we do not need to swear at all—not by God or by heaven or on our own life.

As he has been doing, Jesus continues to address the heart, the inner person, the place from which all things flow. The standard of righteousness in Jesus' day was clear: You can tell lies and not be liable (until you get caught), but if you lie "under oath" you are guilty. Jesus, as always, is aiming for something higher, for a new kind of person with a new kind of character. He is saying, "Under oath or not, those who live in the kingdom can and should tell the truth."

> Have you ever said "I swear" or "I promise" when trying to get others to believe you? Why did you use those words?

BUT WHAT IF I GET CALLED TO BE A WITNESS?

Some Christians have taken Jesus' words about not swearing literally. People like the early Quakers, Leo Tolstoy and the medieval Cathars refused to take an oath, even when forced by the court of law. This resulted in hundreds of Quakers being sent to prison. As much as I respect the early Quakers, I believe they misunderstood what Jesus was saying. Refusing to take an oath is not necessarily radical and could be done with a duplicitous heart intent on defying the system. The radical nature of Jesus' words was not that we should never take an oath but that all of our speech should be honest, genuine, true and trustworthy—a yes that means yes and a no that means no. Jesus says that in the kingdom we are obliged to tell the truth in all circumstances. The kingdom does not run on deception. It simply will not. But this doesn't mean we should never take an oath.

In a court case, should we (as a kingdom-dweller) *refuse* to put our hand on a Bible and swear to tell the truth? Was that Jesus' intent? Absolutely not. That would be just another form of legalism. Jesus is not forbidding us from taking an oath in a court of law, nor is he saying we must never promise we are telling the truth when asked.

> If it's not about not taking oaths, what does it mean, and what impact would it have on our lives if we lived this way?

He is saying, Become the kind of person who naturally tells the truth. Do this often and consistently, and people will not need you to "swear" because you always tell the truth.

AIMING FOR INTEGRITY

Having criticized Quakers for their stance on not taking oaths, I must praise them for getting the *heart* of this passage right in other areas of life. The early Quakers were committed to telling the truth in all matters, which is *the real aim*. They were intent on being people whose word was good, people whose words had integrity. A little known fact is that Quakers are credited with creating the price tag. Prior to the Quakers, all business was done by haggling. The seller set a price higher than the product was worth, and the buyer countered with a lower offer. This went on until an agreement was reached.

The Quakers believed that haggling involved lying. The seller and buyer would name a price they knew was unfair. It may seem like an innocent practice, but haggling did not sit right in the Quakers' hearts. Thus Quakers priced their goods for what they were worth and refused to haggle. They put a price tag on an item and simply refused to negotiate. After a while the idea caught on. It not only saved a lot of time, it also drastically cut down on the number of lies people told every day. Quakers called this "plain speech." Plain speech means speaking without spin or deception. A yes means yes.

HOW LIVING IN THE KINGDOM CAN CURE LYING

Lying always occurs between persons, and we must distinguish between telling something that is false and a lie. Lying is "a false statement made knowingly, with the intent to deceive." Lying is not about the correctness of what a person says but about the intent of the heart. What does living as an apprentice of Jesus, in his glorious kingdom, have to do with lying?

God is truth; he cannot lie (Titus 1:2), and those who follow him must walk and talk in truth. And the Spirit of God not only leads us into truth (John 16:13), but is truth (1 John 5:6). Kingdom people are those who are led by or walk in the Spirit. Therefore, they must walk in truth. The apostle John praised his fellow Christians for doing so: "I was overjoyed when some of the friends arrived and testified to your faithfulness to the truth, namely how you walk in the truth" (3 John 1:3). And Paul urged those under his care always to tell the truth: "So then, putting away falsehood, let all of us speak the truth to our neighbors, for we are members of one another" (Ephesians 4:25).

> How does living in the kingdom help us stop lying to or deceiving others?

This is the baseline, the starting point, for apprentices of Jesus. We begin by "putting away falsehood" (not lying), or in the positive, we speak the truth. We do this because we are "members of one another." Lying to another is lying to myself. Christ dwells in both of us.

People who dwell in the kingdom of heaven will find lying less and less a part of their lives. That is because the kingdom addresses all of the reasons we give for lying. First, in the life with God (the kingdom) we can let go of our fears. We don't need to fear what will happen as long as we are living under his rule and reign. Telling the truth may cause discomfort or embarrassment, but we live with a God who protects us and provides for us. If we choose to lie, we are not in harmony with the kingdom, and losing that is much worse than the consequences of telling the truth.

Understanding our identity in Christ helps us in the area of lying. Paul urged the Colossians, "Do not lie to each other, since you have taken off your old self with its practices" (Colossians 3:9 NIV). Notice the second clause: "since you have taken off the old self." Since Jesus dwells and delights in us, we strive to put an end to deception in our life.

The kingdom is not in trouble. And we who stand in it are never in trouble. Therefore, we can risk telling the truth. We can handle the consequences of the truth. In the kingdom we strive for more than merely not lying. We want our speech to be acceptable not only to the people we address but also to God. The bar is set high. Our words need to be honest and true, but they flow from the heart, so our heart has to be honest and true. At present it may not be, but as long as we keep "pickling" in the kingdom of God, it will be increasingly so. As it becomes genuine and true, so will our words.

IMPROVING OUR SPEECH

I am trying to learn Portuguese because I was privileged to minister alongside Eduardo Pedreira in Brazil, and may do so again in the future. As I write, Eduardo and his wife, Marcia, are in the United States on a sabbatical. They are helping me with my Portuguese, and they are trying to improve their English. We are trying to improve our speech, so we can communicate in other languages. But the most important way we can improve our speech—in any language—is to move beyond trying not to lie by blessing others. One of my favorite verses is Ephesians 4:29: "Let no evil talk come out of your mouths, but only what is useful for building up, as there is need, so that your words may give grace to those who hear" (Ephesians 4:29).

What does "giving grace" in our speech look like? I have coined the following terms to describe ways we give grace through what we say.

Kingdom encouragement. After relating a difficulty I was wrestling with, a friend responded, "Well, remember, God is your shield and banner." Her speech gave me grace by sharing a principle about the kingdom of God; namely, God will stand with us and for us. Her words—just a single sentence—encouraged me.

Kingdom kindness. When I spoke with a friend, who is a true apprentice of Jesus, about an experience of loss and grief, he spoke with amazing sensitivity and gentleness. His kingdom kindness involved reflective feedback, which came from careful listening. It usually involves thoughtful responses and empathetic replies.

These are ways to speak the Golden Rule, saying things to others that we would say to ourselves.

In the kingdom of God we begin by putting away falsehood, but as apprentices of Jesus much more is expected of our speech. Telling the truth is a great start, but as we move further into kingdom living we begin to use our tongues to bless and encourage.

THE LIMITS OF HONESTY

Brad Blanton founded a movement called "Radical Honesty." He has written several books on the subject and offers training seminars to help people learn how to speak the truth in *every* circumstance. Blanton advocates absolute honesty, even if it hurts others. He believes in the importance of truth over all other considerations. Hurt feelings are no reason for lying.

Is Blanton right? Would we all be better off if we told the truth all of the time? To some extent I think he is right. I think we are unduly afraid of the consequences of honesty. And in most cases, honesty is the most loving thing we can do.

But in light of the previous section on blessing and encouraging with our speech, I believe there are limits to honesty. In the movie *A Few Good Men* while under oath a character is pushed to tell the truth and blurts out, "You want the truth? You can't handle the truth!" There are some truths we cannot handle, and do not need to handle. While I am not advocating lying or deception, I believe that loving others (which is the highest goal) may involve not telling someone everything we think or know in every circumstance.

It takes discernment and wisdom to decide when honesty is helpful and when it's harmful. For me, a serious "heart check" is necessary when I am in these situations. I pray for the people involved before I speak. I want my words to come from a kingdom attitude—which is love. Paul said, "Speaking the truth in love, we must grow up in every way into him who is the head, into Christ" (Ephesians 4:15). That is a great phrase: *speaking the truth in love*. And love is willing the good of another. Sometimes "willing the good" will mean telling the unvarnished truth. At other times it may mean withholding the truth. The issue is not easy, but fortunately we have prayer and the Holy Spirit to guide us.

MY SCARLET LETTER

I have thought a lot about the night I let a person assume I had read *The Scarlet Letter*. I think I lied because I wanted to fit in. I wanted to be liked. I might have looked unintelligent if I had said, "No, I have not read that book." I felt so guilty that I felt as if I needed to wear a scarlet *L* to let others know of my sin. I have since repented of this practice.

Now I routinely say, "No, I am totally unfamiliar with that." One time I was asked if I understood a certain theory on something, and at first I thought I did, but when I realized I did not, I stopped the person and said, "Excuse me, but now that I know what you are talking about, I must admit that I am not familiar with it." To my surprise, the person did not think less of me. In fact, he said, "I admire you for telling the truth." That is the paradox of honesty. In the end we do not seem foolish, we seem genuine, which is a lot more important to people than trying to impress them.

When we know who we are (people in whom Christ dwells) and where we live (in the kingdom of God) we are more able to be straightforward, simple, clear and honest. As long as our hearts are good and we intend no malice, we are in a position to put away falsehood and offer plain speech to others. Beyond that, we can use our speech to give grace to people, which is one of the reasons God gave us the ability to speak. We can learn how to let our yes be yes and also to bless.

silence

Those who live a monastic life (monks and nuns) regularly practice the discipline of silence. They do so for many reasons, but one is to counter the sins of the tongue, such as lying or gossip. Practicing this discipline teaches them the power of words and gives them greater control over their tongues. Most of us are not monks or nuns, but we can also practice this discipline to help us learn how to bridle our tongues.

If we do not speak, we cannot lie. We cannot gossip. We cannot hurt others with our words. So, we practice silence to have better control over our tongues. We will not become proficient overnight, but in time (as with all of the tools we use) we will see progress.

There are two exercises to choose from this week. The main exercise is a very challenging discipline, one which needs a lot of preparation.

GOING A DAY WITHOUT WORDS

The first exercise is to *go a day without speaking*. This is the primary spiritual tool this week, so if you can only do one of the two, do this one. It is very challenging and takes a lot of planning and preparation.

In our world, how is this possible?

First, choose a day when this will be less of a problem for you. For many, the weekend works best. You can choose to go from sundown to sundown, Friday evening to Saturday evening, for example.

Some warnings:

1. Be sure to let others know you are doing this. Silence creates suspicion and concern. People will ask whether you are OK. If someone calls you and you do not respond, they may get unnecessarily concerned. Thus you may want to send an email or a text message to your family and friends to let them know what you are doing.

2. If you are asked to speak and it is beneficial to do so, then speak. Charity overrides all discipline. If someone is about to be hit by a bus, by all means yell.

3. In many cases, you can use hand gestures or written notes if you feel you must communicate. Tip: *keep a notepad around so that you can communicate with others when necessary.* (However, this does not include texting!)

Most people find this to be a wonderful experience. Don't be afraid of it. Be aware of speech and of people and things around you, which increase dramatically.

GOING A DAY WITHOUT LYING

For some, the first exercise is an impossibility. If that is the case, then choose one day this week to be a "Lie-Free Day." Do your very best not to lie to anyone for an entire day. If you do lie, try your best to correct it on the spot. Simply say, "You know, what I said was not true. The truth is . . ." You may be afraid people will be upset or disappointed with you, but I have found the opposite. Most people find it refreshing. And correcting yourself will help prevent the next lie.

seven

Learning to Bless
Those who curse us

My friend Jane is a women's college basketball coach and has been so most of her life. She has been remarkably successful, amassing over four hundred NCAA Division I wins. She is one of the most dedicated Christ-followers I have known. Before each game Jane writes K.C. on her hand, which stands for Kingdom Coach. She says she does it to remind herself who she is and where she is. I marvel at how she goes about her job as a coach from the perspective of the kingdom of God. In essence Jane asks, How would Jesus function if he were a college basketball coach?

Over time Jane found ways to do that. She let go of anger and the need to retaliate. She lived with honesty and integrity. Her players, her bosses, the fans and the media all loved her. She was a light to her world. Then suddenly, in her third year with a new team, her team began to lose. They ended up near the bottom of their division. Soon the media began to point fingers at her, even wondering aloud if it was time for a new coach. Eventually they issued a direct call for her to be fired.

Ironically, one of the sportswriters who had been the most critical of her coaching phoned her one day to ask for a large favor. What nerve, after publicly denouncing her! But Jane told me, "I decided not to hold a grudge. He is just doing his job. And I live in the kingdom, so I decided to bless someone who cursed me." The next year there were some wonderful moments for her team, but the win-loss column was the same, and she was asked to resign.

When I heard the news, I made the call I had prayed I would never have to make. Jane was obviously hurt, and it was clear she had been crying. There were many things I wanted to say, but I took a deep breath and said the only thing I knew to be absolutely true: "Just remember, Jane, the kingdom is not in trouble, and Jane is not in trouble." What was most impressive was the fact that she had followed Jesus' teaching, never attacking those who had attacked her, and instead, blessing and praying for them.

FALSE NARRATIVE: HIT BACK HARDER

In the kingdom of this world, people feel disempowered, vulnerable, impotent and exposed. The quickest way to deal with this insecurity is to gain power, to take charge. Feeling weak? Go to the gym and build muscles. Feeling financially vulnerable? Build wealth. Feeling unfairly treated by others? Fight back, take them to court, assert your rights. The dominant narrative is, *If someone hits you, hit them back harder.*

Much bloodshed stems from this narrative. Protestants and Catholics in Northern Ireland, Jews and Arabs in the West Bank, Hutus and Tutsis in Rwanda live with this ideology: use force and retaliate in order to protect yourself. It goes back to childhood playgrounds. When I was about nine, a thirteen-year-old bully pushed around all of the younger kids. He stole our money, took our sports equipment and knocked us to the ground just for fun. When I told my dad, he said, "Well, someone has to stand up to him." I was actually a bit of a fighter in those days, so I took my dad's advice to heart. The next day I did not back down, which led to a fight. I surprised the bully by holding my own. Though I did not win, I also did not lose, and I knew that he would never bother me again. He didn't.

This embedded a false narrative in my mind: the only way to protect yourself is to use force and violence. Like using guilt to shape behavior, using force works in the short run but does not produce lasting change. And worse, it usually leads to more violence. When faced with injustice, whether it be public shaming, unfair treatment or intentional harm, the natural reaction is to demand "an eye for an eye." But as Gandhi once said, "An eye for an eye makes the whole world blind."

What childhood experiences taught you to use force and violence to protect yourself?

KINGDOM JUJITSU
The next section of the Sermon on the Mount contains some of the most challenging and demanding requirements of those who want to live as Jesus' apprentices.

> You have heard that it was said, "An eye for an eye and a tooth for a tooth." But I say to you, Do not resist an evildoer. But if anyone strikes you on the right cheek, turn the other also; and if anyone wants to sue you and take your coat, give your cloak as well; and if anyone forces you to go one mile, go also the second mile. Give to everyone who begs from you, and do not refuse anyone who wants to borrow from you. (Matthew 5:38-42)

Jesus is once again offering a contrast ("You have heard . . . but I say . . ."). He is reminding us of the common teaching about justice, namely, "an eye for an eye," which is "the law of reciprocity." The law of reciprocity, or *lex talionis*, was understood by everyone: "Anyone who maims another shall suffer the same injury in return: fracture for fracture, eye for eye, tooth for tooth; the injury inflicted is the injury to be suffered" (Leviticus 24:19-20). Reciprocity was the standard of rightness, fairness and justice.

Lex talionis is good for a society because it prevents people from the natural tendency to do *more* damage in retaliation: "the injury inflicted is the injury to be suffered." The common course would work like this: "If you kill my dog, I will kill your dog and your cows and your chickens—I will show you not to mess with me!" You can see why those who kept the law of reciprocity felt they were being good and right. They would have liked to do much more. By not overretaliating they were being just.

> Can you think of a situation in your life when you wanted to overretaliate?

Jesus is teaching us that in the kingdom of God there is a better, higher way than *lex talionis*. He gives four concrete examples of injustice and reveals how those in the kingdom of God ought to react. This way of responding to injustice reminds me of *jujitsu*. Jujitsu is a martial art, and many think of it as a form of fighting. However, the word means "a way of yielding" by using an attacker's force and energy to work against him or her. Instead of trying to match force with force, jujitsu teaches a person how to overcome an armed opponent with no other weapons than intelligence.

That is precisely what Jesus is teaching. Unless we understand this principle, this passage may cause a great deal of harm. People conclude that Jesus is teaching us to become passive victims of abuses. A closer look, though, shows that Jesus is offering a brilliant way to respond to abuse and attack from a position of kingdom security. In each of the four illustrations Jesus teaches the same thing: in the kingdom of God we do not need to retaliate, because there is a better way.

1. Someone attacks or insults us. "If anyone strikes you on the right cheek, turn the other also" (v. 39). In Jesus' day it was common to see a master slapping a slave. A master could treat a slave any way he or she wanted. But a person could never slap someone in a higher rank. Because the left hand was never used for hitting, to slap someone on the right cheek meant hitting that person with the back of the right hand. Usually when this happened, the slave would cower in submission. This allowed the abuse to continue. A slave could hit the person back, but with grave consequences. If a person of the same social rank was struck, he or she could take the offender to court. Slapping was a punishable offense in Jesus' day. Jesus, however, offers a stunning idea: offer the left cheek.

In effect, doing this would leave the striker wondering what to do next. That is kingdom jujitsu. People of the kingdom have an alternative to retaliating or litigating. They can choose a nonviolent, even yielding approach. In so doing the aggressor might—or might not— wake up to the wrongness of the act; the person would have to think twice about hitting again.

Of course, we can't turn this into a law: apprentices of Jesus should never let people simply abuse them. That is precisely the kind of legalism Jesus has been criticizing (the righteousness of the scribes and the Pharisees). There can and will be times when we need to protect ourselves. Jesus is not giving a universal law but a kingdom principle that offers an alternative to the way people react to each other in the world. When we are in a stable place (the kingdom) with a solid identity (one in whom Christ dwells and delights) we can choose to respond to attack by not attacking back.

2. Someone sues us for what is rightfully theirs. "If anyone wants to sue you and take your coat, give your cloak as well" (v. 40). In Jesus' day, the poor were often at the mercy of the rich. Many people were so poor that they had nothing but their clothing. If they borrowed money from the rich, they would use their clothes as collateral, the most common being the tunic (wrongly translated here by the NRSV as "coat"), a garment worn over the skin. A lender could ask for the money to be repaid at any time, and if the poor person could not pay it back, the lender could sue to keep the tunic. That would leave the poor person with his outer coat (NRSV's "cloak"), which allowed him to have something to wear. Technically this would be fair. But in reality, the entire system was unfair and oppressive.

Jesus once again offers a stunning solution: offer your outer coat as well. This would be totally unnecessary, far beyond the legal demand of the lender. Even more, cloaks (coats) often doubled as a blanket, and there was a law (Exodus 22:25-27) that prohibited taking another person's cloak. Why does Jesus say to offer it freely? Because the guiding principle of the kingdom is love. If someone takes something from us, the normal reaction is to cling to it. Those who understand kingdom provision are able to take a different approach: "Here is my shirt. Do you need my coat as well?"

Once again, we must not make this into a law. It is an inner attitude, not a commandment. If someone asks us for something, we are not required to give them something else in addition. Jesus is illustrating a unique response to a request. Love is the great commandment of the kingdom, and love always asks how we may help the other. Because we are not in a position of scarcity, we can freely give of our possessions.

3. Someone imposes on us. "If anyone forces you to go one mile, go also the second mile" (v. 41). In Jesus' day, if a Roman soldier asked a Jew to carry his luggage, the Jew would have to carry that luggage up to one mile. Notice he says "*forces* you to go one mile." No Jew would want to serve the hated Romans. Knowing that the soldiers might abuse this right, the Romans enacted a law that made it illegal for a soldier to force a Jew to carry his bags indefinitely. So they settled on the "one mile" amount. Once again, Jesus is asking his apprentices to do the unthinkable: go two miles. This is not like picking up a hitchhiker or helping a friend move. The person we are assisting is not asking for help; we are being forced to help.

Jesus offers more surprising counsel: go the second mile. Why? Because the guiding principle in the kingdom of God is love, and love seeks the good of the other. Those who lack a giving heart would go one mile begrudgingly and not a step farther. Those who live in the kingdom can say, "Do you need me to carry this farther?" In the kingdom the recurrent question is "How can I help you?" which even extends to those we find offensive.

4. Someone begs from us. "Give to everyone who begs from you, and do not refuse anyone who wants to borrow from you" (v. 42). In Jesus' culture the dominant teaching about giving money was: give only to kinsmen, and even then give the minimum.

> If there is among you anyone in need, a member of your community in any of your towns within the land that the LORD your God is giving you, do not be hard-hearted or tight-fisted toward your needy neighbor. You should rather open your hand, willingly lending enough to meet the need, whatever it may be. (Deuteronomy 15:7-8)

According to the law, giving should be for people in our community, and only to meet what is needed. Everyone was aware of this teaching. Jesus, however, removes these restrictions. He does not stipulate that giving should be for someone we know, and he puts no limit on giving.

Asking and giving are acts of vulnerability. People in need must humble themselves, and those asked to give must let go of our resources. *Does the person who asks us for money really need it? Are they lazy? Am I enabling them? And if I give to that person will I have less money for myself?* Begging requires great humility; giving freely requires great trust. In the kingdom of God we stand secure and can sacrifice without fearing we will be abused.

Once again, this is not a law. There are times it is unwise to give without stipulation. My bishop, Scott Jones, told me about a time when he was walking on a street in London and a woman with a small child asked him for money for food. He gave her the money and walked on. Then he decided to follow her to see if she really would buy food. The woman went right to a liquor store and bought alcohol.

Bishop Jones concluded, "I decided never to give money in that way. Instead, I give money to relief organizations who have ways of making sure money gets to the right people for the right needs." That is one solution.

In all four situations Jesus asks his apprentices to do the unnatural and the unthinkable. The world imposes natural boundaries (fines for cheek slapping, limits on litigation, predetermined distances, and restrictions on giving) to obtain justice and prevent abuse. But the kingdom of God aims higher than justice. We are in a different position when we stand in the kingdom of God. Practicing kingdom jujitsu startles people and provokes them to ask, What kind of person would do such a thing? This is evangelism at its best.

> Have you ever seen someone apply kingdom jijitsu? How did it affect the people involved?

LOVE YOUR ENEMIES
Jesus' Sermon continues:

> You have heard that it was said, "You shall love your neighbor and hate your enemy." But I say to you, Love your enemies and pray for those who persecute you, so that you may be children of your Father in heaven; for he makes his sun rise on the evil and on the good, and sends rain on the righteous and on the unrighteous. For if you love those who love you, what reward do you have? Do not even the tax collectors do the same? And if you greet only your brothers and sisters, what more are you doing than others? Do not even the Gentiles do the same? Be perfect, therefore, as your heavenly Father is perfect. (Matthew 5:43-48)

The law of the limits of love and the right to vengeance was clear and familiar to all Jews, coming straight from Leviticus: "You shall not take vengeance or bear a grudge against any of your people, but you shall love your neighbor as yourself: I am the LORD" (Leviticus 19:18).

Loving your neighbor was the basic expectation, the minimum standard, in the same way that giving money to your kin was a basic requirement of the law. But if a person was not your neighbor or kin, then you were not obligated to love him or her. And it was perfectly acceptable to hate your enemies. These were the dominant narratives of those who listened to the Sermon.

But Jesus asks for much more. He commands his people to love their enemies. What does it mean to love someone? To most people love is a feeling, an emotion. But the Greek word *agapao* (or *agape*) refers not to a feeling but to an action. To love (*agapao*) is *to will the good of another*. It does not entail an emotion, loving or even liking a person. We will their good and demonstrate it in action. This is a crucial point. Loving our enemies seems impossible to us because we think, *I can never feel love for a person who abuses me.* Jesus is not asking his apprentices to *feel* love but to *act* in love toward everyone, including our enemies.

> Can you think of individuals you don't *feel* love toward, but whom you could *will their good?* How might willing their good change your relationship with them?

It's easy to love those who love us: even the tax collectors do that. It is hard to love those who would harm us. It's easy to pray for people we love, but not for those who persecute us. Nonetheless, it can be done. And when we do, we are behaving as our Father in heaven (Matthew 5:44). God loves his enemies by acting for their good.

> But God proves his love for us in that while we still were sinners Christ died for us. . . . For if while we were enemies, we

were reconciled to God through the death of his Son, much more surely, having been reconciled, will we be saved by his life. (Romans 5:8, 10)

When we love our enemies, we are acting like our Father and Jesus.

PUTTING ON THE CHARACTER OF CHRIST

Jesus practiced what he preached. He was beaten and spit on, yet he did not retaliate. He was tortured and did not lash out. He loved people who hated him and forgave the people who executed him. Jesus is not asking us to do something he himself would not do. He invites us to a way of living that transcends the normal course of action. Again, outside of the kingdom and without the strength of the indwelling Christ, we cannot do this. In our own flesh (sarx) we do not have the capacity to behave in these extraordinary ways. However, we follow an extraordinary God who offers extraordinary resources.

In what ways have you felt the indwelling Christ give you the strength to follow his example?

David Augsburger observes, "[Jesus] chose the way of the cross as the clearest expression of how God confronts and deals with human evil, not by responding in kind, giving evil for evil, but by extending self-giving, nonresistant love." Jesus' apprentices refuse to use violence not because of an abstract principle but because we are his disciples; we do things as he did. We do what he taught in order to become the kind of person he was.

Every time we retaliate we are operating by the narratives of the kingdom of this world. Each time we curse our enemies we are affirming our faith in the narratives of the life without God. When we refuse to freely give, we demonstrate our allegiance to the world's narratives of scarcity and fear. When we hate our enemies we betray the God who loves his enemies. Conversely, when we pray for and bless those who curse us, we align ourselves with God and his king-dom. We are doing what Jesus did.

MORE THAN ENOUGH PEOPLE

To cross the bridge from selfishness to generosity we need even more than new narratives; we will need the power of the indwelling Christ. In two beautiful passages Miroslav Volf explains how Christians are "more than enough" people:

> If we are indwelled by Christ who became poor that we can become rich, we will be rich. No matter how little we have, we will be "more than enough" people. . . . And yet, without being "more than enough" people, our wanting will always outpace our having, and we'll end up perpetually exhausted and forever dissatisfied.

We are "more than enough" people not because of the size of our bank account or the number of our accomplishments, but because Christ dwells in us. Our value is immense, and our world is safe, safe for us to give and to sacrifice our resources.

Outside of the kingdom we are not-enough people, always search-ing for our identity and happiness in material things; our "wanting will always outpace our having." Volf describes the one indwelt by Christ as "a rich self":

> A rich self looks toward the future with trust. It gives rather than holding things back in fear of coming out too short, because it believes God's promise that God will take care of it. Finite and endangered, a rich self still gives, because its life is "hidden with Christ" in the infinite, unassailable, and utterly generous God, the Lord of the present, the past, and the future.

The spiritually rich self is a "more than enough" person who is con-scious of being indwelt by Christ. Such a person is able to cross the bridge from self-centeredness to generosity because there is no fear of coming out short. God is with us and for us and able to provide for us.

God is with us—so the need to retaliate is diminished. God has an endless supply of resources—so the need to hang on to possessions decreases. God is looking out for our needs—so we can take the time to go the extra mile. God is the real owner of all we have—so the need to hoard and protect it diminishes. Kingdom *identity* (I am one in whom Christ dwells) and kingdom *awareness* (I am in the strong and secure kingdom of God) are the keys to doing what Jesus calls us to do. With these we can learn how to become radically generous and to live extraordinary lives.

> Has there been a time when you were a "more than enough" person? If so, how did it feel, and how did your behavior change?

DARE TO BE EXTRAORDINARY

Jesus is calling his apprentices to be extraordinary. Earlier in the Sermon he told us we could become the salt of the earth and light of the world. He urges us to live with a higher standard than mere justice. He calls us to live by the law of love. He tells us that in so doing we become "perfect" as our heavenly Father is perfect (Matthew 5:48). The word *perfect* causes a problem for many of us because we think it means moral flawlessness, which we know is impossible. The Greek word used here is *teleios*, which refers to a kind of spiritual maturity. We should not expect to be able to fulfill all that Jesus is asking of us right away. Maturity takes time. But we must give the kingdom of God a chance to operate in our lives. The following are three stories of people who dared to be extraordinary.

Pope John Paul.

In May 1981, the late Pope John Paul II was shot when Mohammed Agca attempted to take his life. Some two years later, reported Lance Morrow, in a bare, white-walled cell in Rome's Rebibba prison, John Paul tenderly held the hand that held the gun that was meant to kill him. For 21 minutes, the Pope sat with his would-be assassin. . . . The two talked softly. Once or twice, Agca laughed. The Pope forgave him for the shooting. At the end of the meeting, Agca either kissed the Pope's ring or pressed the Pope's hand to his forehead in a Muslim gesture of respect.

Steven.

Steven's son Bobby was killed in the September 11 attacks. Steven speaks wearing his son's baseball cap. He shares the pain and anger that the senseless death of his son has caused. But he also says, "But there has not been a moment that passed when I believed that more violence will solve anything. I do not want any father to feel what I feel right now." Steven started a group called "Families for Peaceful Tomorrows," whose slogan is, "Our grief is not a cry for war."

The mothers of Boyle Heights.

In the early 1990s, gang violence erupted in Boyle Heights, a section of East Los Angeles. Eight gangs were in conflict in the parish around the Dolores Mission Catholic Church. Killings and injuries happened daily. A group of women who met for prayer read together the story of Jesus walking on water (Matt. 14:22-33). Then one of the mothers, electrified by the text, began to identify the parallels between the Jesus story and her own.

The gang warfare in Boyle Heights was the storm on the sea of Galilee; the people hiding behind locked doors were the disciples huddled in the storm; the crackle of gunfire was the lightning; in both cases death was imminent. Then Jesus appeared and they hoped for a magical rescue. Instead, he said, "Get out of the boat." "Walk on the water." "Enter the violence." . . .

That night, seventy women began a *peregrinación*, a procession from one barrio to another. They brought food, guitars and love. As they ate chips and salsa and drank Cokes with gang members, they began to sing the old songs of Jalisco, Chiapas, and Michoacán. The gang members were disoriented, baffled; the war zones were silent.

Each night the mothers walked. By nonviolently intruding and intervening they "broke the rules of war." The old script of retaliation and escalating violence was challenged and changed. It is no accident that the women christened their nighttime journeys "love walks."

As the relationships between the women and the gang members grew, the kids told their stories. Anguish over lack of jobs; anger at police brutality; rage over the hopelessness of poverty. Together they developed a tortilla factory, a bakery, a child-care center, a job-training program, a class on conflict-resolution techniques, a school for further learning, a neighborhood group to monitor and report police misbehavior, and more.

And it began with the challenges "Get out of the boat" and "Walk on water."

What I love about these stories is how they bear witness to God. We behave this way because God behaves this way. God loves his enemies and forgives those who hate him. We conform to this reality over time, and should not expect overnight change. In time we learn to love and pray for those we once thought of as competitors, and perhaps one day we will face our enemies and be able to wish them well.

In what ways have you already started to resemble God?

A KINGDOM COACH

I opened with a story about my friend Jane, who was fired yet dealt with those who criticized her with kingdom aplomb. It did not take long for her to find another coaching job. Halfway through her first season with her new team she sent me the following email:

Good morning Jim, in whom Christ dwells . . .

Well, you lived with me through the hard times, and you taught me how to navigate in the world as a Kingdom coach, so I had to share this with you. I hope it brings you joy.

My new team has played pretty well off and on this season. We won some, and we lost some. Then we faced the #7 team in the nation. Well, I have had moments when I felt God was with me as a coach before, but this was different. I didn't let anything bother me and felt so much a desire to be like Jesus . . . the original Kingdom coach. On game day I spent a lot of time in prayer— it had been a long time since I had been in a big game on television. But I was relaxed . . . felt good with the kids. A lot happened along the way, but to make a long story short, we won!

Our university has never beaten a team ranked that high in their entire history. The fans there were so, so happy and my kids were screaming . . . full of joy . . . and I had an overwhelming emotion . . . of gratitude . . . not revenge for what people had said and done to me, but thankfulness to JESUS . . . giver of all things.

Jim, I have won some huge games in my life, but this was different. I felt deep in the Kingdom of God, and it felt better than any win ever did before. I did not need any affirmation, nor feel the need to prove my worth, because I knew the truth of who I am and where I am, and it is my core value now. Thanks for the wisdom and teaching . . .

Keeping the faith
Jane in whom Christ dwells

After reading it I opened my tattered copy of Dallas Willard's *Divine Conspiracy* and read these words aloud from a page I had dog-eared long ago, because they reminded me of what Jane had experienced. Dallas is describing how those who live in the kingdom of God find comfort, even in trial, and stand firm when under duress:

> We know that we will be taken care of, no matter what. We can be vulnerable because we are, in the end, simply invulnerable. And once we have broken the power of anger and desire over our lives, we know that the way of Christ in response to personal injury and imposition is always the easier way. It is the only way that allows us to move serenely in the midst of the harm and beyond it.

Jane is living proof that the kingdom is never in trouble, and neither are those who dwell in it.

praying for the success of competitors

Most of us will not be slapped or sued this week, and hopefully none of us will be cursed or persecuted. For this reason we can easily sidestep this section of the Sermon on the Mount and think, *Good thing I don't have to turn my cheek or offer my accuser my whole wardrobe.* But the core teaching is to begin seeing those who are a threat to us in a different light. Instead of retaliating, Jesus is asking us to bless those who harm us. It might be a good practice to think of someone who is your enemy—someone who you know is actively pursuing your demise. Many of us will be hard-pressed to come up with an authentic enemy.

So I would like you to scale it down a little and take a smaller step in obeying Jesus commands. I want you to pray for the success of a competitor. A competitor is anyone you are measured against, *anyone whose success in some way diminishes yours.* It might be a business competitor or someone you compete against in school or in sports. Perhaps it is a parent whose child competes with your child in athletics or the fine arts. If you are a pastor, you might want to pray for the success of nearby churches.

Ask God to reveal these people or institutions to you.

Some have said to me, "To be honest, I really do not have any competitors." If that is the case, think of someone who causes difficulty in your life. My wife calls these people "irregular persons"—people who get under our skin or do things that causes us problems. Choose a competitor or difficult person. Pray for guidance from the Holy Spirit about who you should pray for.

It usually doesn't take long to figure out which persons or institutions are our competitors, but once we begin praying for them we notice an inner tension; namely, we don't really *want* them to succeed. At first we merely say it and don't necessarily feel it. That is OK. Be at peace about this. This is a slow process. As we do it over time we will begin to notice our feelings change. Whenever I engage in this exercise something strange happens. I won't tell you what that is. You will soon discover it for yourself. And when you do, you'll appreciate the wisdom of Jesus and his command to pray for your enemies.

In terms of actual practice, how exactly do we do this? The following are a few tips that I have found helpful.

- Spend a few minutes each day praying for your competitor, asking God to bless him or her and the work he or she does.

- Hold that person or institution up before God, and pray for as many good things to happen as you can think of.

- Do this once a day for four or five days this week. See if your heart begins to change toward this person.

eight

Learning to Live
without Vainglory

I was invited to speak at a Christian university chapel for three consecutive days. Known as an outstanding academic college, it attracts a lot of bright students. Its chapel program is well known for having some of the best speakers and musicians as weekly guests. It holds around twenty-five hundred students, who must go to chapel a few times a week. It was an honor to be asked to speak for three days. I was both eager and intimidated. Earlier in the semester Billy Graham had stood in the same pulpit; the week after I was to speak the stage would be inhabited by the most popular Christian band in the country at the time. I felt unworthy.

The first day I spoke went pretty well. I discovered that the students and I had something in common: we wanted to be high achievers for God, which means we tended toward legalism. I shared my own story, and it seemed to connect with them. I also shared my discovery of the unconditional love of God, the antidote to legalism. My talk on the second day went even better. But I felt a tremendous inner burden: I wanted to be liked, to impress the students and the faculty, to leave the school as a winner. And yet my only real reason for being there was to speak words of encouragement, to point people to God, to let the words of my mouth and the meditations of my heart be a blessing to the students. The conflict did not go away.

Before I spoke on the third day, I spent time in prayer and let the matter go. I wanted to help the students, and I stepped up to the microphone with a pure desire to be an instrument of God and nothing more. I thought about each student's pain and uncertainty, struggles and fears, and I wanted to bring a word of comfort and encouragement from God. I found myself speaking from a very deep place that morning, with courage, conviction and passion. When I was done I thanked them for listening to me and then gave an actor's bow to show my gratitude.

The students began to applaud. Though I was looking down, I noticed that the applause got louder. When I looked up, they were standing. *Wow*, I thought, *these students are awfully polite*. I walked to the chair where I had been sitting, and the university president leaned over to me and whispered, "You should soak this in because they very seldom give standing ovations." Suddenly a feeling of elation and exhilaration coursed through my body.

As I drove home I still felt my internal struggle. I went to the college with a mixture of motives. I wanted to do ministry, to bless and encourage students. I also wanted to be liked, to be well received and to impress people. I have heard that a person's heart is truly in the kingdom of God when, after speaking, his or her desire is not for people to say, "What a great preacher," but rather, "What a great God he (or she) knows." I thought about the pull of pride, the desire for accolades and the longing for compliments—where that comes from and how we can let it go in the kingdom. Even though I have not mastered it, I now have a better sense of what makes us want others to think well of us, and how we can prevent that desire from ruling in our hearts.

FALSE NARRATIVE: MY VALUE IS DETERMINED BY YOUR ASSESSMENT

The narrative that gives rise to our need for affirmation is a story we learn early in our lives. When we do well, we receive affirmation; when we do poorly, we receive no affirmation, and may be criticized. "You ate all of your peas—you are so good." Or "You did not finish your peas—off to your room, and no dessert!" Life continues this way at each phase, from school to sports to jobs. Do great things and your value increases; fail and your value decreases. Over time we begin to hunger for others' affirmation because it seems to establish our value. Positive appraisal can become more important than actually being good or doing well.

We all want to be loved. We all long to feel that we are valuable, worthwhile and wonderful. In a sense we are. Regardless of our physical appearance, talents or abilities, we are amazing beings created in the image of God. But the world will not tell us this. Too seldom do we hear it from our parents or our loved ones. Even our churches contribute to this problem. We praise success and lionize certain people for their piety. Though there is nothing wrong with acknowledging a ministry success or a godly person, the narrative that value is determined by success may continue to work its way in peoples' minds.

How does vainglory get ahold of us, and how can we combat it?

The world measures our worth on the basis of our appearance, production and performance—which seem to be the only things that count. This narrative says our value is determined by others' assessment. If they say we are good, then we are. Image is everything in our world. We feel the need to be appreciated, respected, applauded and affirmed for what we do. Then we feel good about ourselves. The need for love is temporarily assuaged by admiration; it is the only substitute we can find. Unfortunately, admiration based on our looks or performance is fickle and fleeting. We are only as good as our next performance.

VAINGLORY: THE EIGHTH DEADLY SIN

Throughout the Sermon Jesus moves us along a continuum, beginning with the pervasive problem of anger, culminating in the challenge to love and bless our enemies. If we make it this far we have gone a long way to becoming a whole person. Yet Jesus knows we are not done yet. There is yet another heart problem that plagues people in their attempts to grow closer to God. The early Christian teachers and writers used a word that perfectly described this problem: *vainglory*. Though most of us are familiar with the seven deadly sins, the Orthodox Church speaks of eight deadly sins, adding vainglory to the list. Vainglory is essentially rooted in insecurity and is driven by our need for affirmation by others. It is very subtle and hard to detect.

When I went to the college to speak I wanted them to think, *Jim is a really terrific speaker and a humble guy as well.* That response would make me feel really good about myself. My worth would be established by their affirmation. Conversely, if I had not gotten a positive response (which has happened many times) my value would be in question. This example is appropriate because vainglory, while a problem for everyone, is a particular problem for religious people.

A SUBTLE TRAP FOR RELIGIOUS PEOPLE

Outside of the kingdom of God, we have no way to determine our value other than what others say about us. If we do something well and no one notices, it drives us crazy because we have lost the thing we want the most—affirmation and praise. It's easy to see how we transfer this narrative into our religious lives. Most people praise religious activities. Thus spiritually mature people, those who pray and read their Bibles and fast, often receive accolades, which tempts them to vainglory. And this also affects those who do not struggle with the vices such as anger, lust and lying. Vainglory is the bane of the pious.

John Cassian, a church father, wrote "One who would not be taken in by the vices of the flesh can be all the more vulnerable to vain-glory." Because they are not defeated by the more "carnal sins," they might be tempted to think they are better than others, that their spiritual lives are superior to those who fail in obvious ways.

When the devil sees someone who is serious about his or her spiritual life, he does not give up. He utilizes a special vice to destroy them: vainglory. Religiously challenged people usually don't struggle with vainglory. They know they are not spiritually proficient, that their moral character is not impressive. But the temptation to vainglory knocks at the door of the pious and pure each day, and it can create a life that looks bright on the outside but is dark on the inside. Andrew Murray wrote, "There is no pride so dangerous, so subtle and insidious, as the pride of holiness."

Vainglory is the most elusive of the vices we have addressed so far. It hides under the guise of virtue: "This disease strikes precisely where a man's virtue lies." This is the only vice that actually *needs* a virtue in order to exist. Vainglory hides behind another virtue, which makes it difficult to see. In the bragging Christmas letter the author is alerting us to success after success—all good things. What could be wrong with that? Nothing. Except that in many cases the true intent of the author is to impress the reader with how wonderful his or her family is. No one ever writes about strain in the marriage, that a child is in therapy for an anxiety disorder, or that a family member came in last in a vocal contest. We don't hear about the suffering, the failing or the struggles, only the accomplishments.

Vainglory appears in my life many ways. In each of the following examples you will notice something good as well as something bad:

- Whenever I accomplish something or receive accolades for something I have done, I immediately want to let others know.

- I try to keep others from knowing my weaknesses and failings. This is just as much about vainglory as broadcasting my successes. In both cases I am seeking to have others think well of me.

- In most conversations I try to appear humble, and yet I very much want the other person to know how wonderful I am. And if that does not appear to be happening I find subtle ways to interject my accomplishments. If I do it well, they will not even notice.

- I am not above dropping names. All of my close friends are well aware of all of the famous people I have met or spent time with.

- Nearly every act of service I have ever done has become known to others—and I have never hindered these from being known.

- When watching my kids perform in sports or the arts, I find myself sometimes more interested in them performing well in front of others than I am in their own enjoyment of the game or the show.

Just when we might begin to think, *Well, I have conquered anger, lust and lying, and have learned to bless those who curse me—I am really something now!* we find that we have another obstacle in the road to kingdom living: vainglory—the need to have others think well of us in order to feel worthy.

> Jesus was critical of three vainglorious acts (ostentatious giving, praying and fasting) that were common in his day. What are some modern illustrations of vainglory we see in our churches?

JESUS' NARRATIVE

Jesus deals with vainglory in one of the larger sections of the Sermon on the Mount. He gives three examples of people doing good things with the intention of being praised by others, using pious behavior as a cloak to conceal it. Three religious activities that we engage in will likely make others think well of us: giving alms, prayer and fasting. All three are God-given disciplines that when done rightly tune our hearts to God's kingdom. However, they can be done in such a way that they actually harm us. Jesus shows his deep understanding of the human heart:

Beware of practicing your piety before others in order to be seen by them; for then you will have no reward from your Father in heaven.

So whenever you give alms, do not sound a trumpet before you, as the hypocrites do in the synagogues and in the streets, so that they may be praised by others. Truly I tell you, they have received their reward. But when you give alms, do not let your left hand know what your right hand is doing, so that your alms may be in secret; and your Father who sees in secret will reward you.

And whenever you pray, do not be like the hypocrites; for they love to stand and pray in the synagogues and at the street corners, so that they may be seen by others. Truly I tell you, they have received their reward. But whenever you pray, go into your room and shut the door and pray to your Father who is in secret; and your Father who sees in secret will reward you.

When you are praying do not heap up empty phrases as the Gentiles do; for they think that they will be heard because of their many words. Do not be like them, for your Father knows what you need before you ask him.

And whenever you fast, do not look dismal, like the hypocrites, for they disfigure their faces so as to show others that they are fasting. Truly I tell you, they have received their reward. But when you fast, put oil on your head and wash your face, so that your fasting may be seen not by others but by your Father who is in secret; and your Father who sees in secret will reward you. (Matthew 6:1-8, 16-18)

I will try to explain this passage in its original context to help explain what Jesus was condemning.

First, Jesus describes a common practice when giving alms (money given to the poor). The synagogue in the first century had a system in place to care for the poor, much like a welfare state. People gave a portion of their money to the synagogue, which was then given to the needy. When someone gave a significant gift, it was common for that to be acknowledged in the synagogue (Sirach 31:11). There is nothing wrong with giving money to people in need; in fact, it is a good and godly thing to do. And there is nothing wrong with having others acknowledge the gift. Jesus is not criticizing the act of public acknowledgment. He is asking whether we gave that gift in order to be praised by others. If so, then we already have what we asked for.

Have you ever been tempted to let others know about your good works?

Second, Jesus describes another scene common in his day: prayer in the synagogues and on the street corners. Devout Jews prayed three times a day, often in public. At the ninth hour people often went to their synagogue to pray, and they commonly prayed aloud while standing. So it was obvious when a person was praying. Again, there is nothing wrong with going to a religious place for prayer. But Jesus asks what we are seeking. Do we want people to see us praying so that they will think we are pious and godly? If so, we have what we seek.

Third, Jesus describes the common practice of fasting. The Pharisees fasted twice a week (see Luke 18:12), usually on Mondays and Thursdays. Some people wore sackcloth or mourning clothes. They often put dust and ashes on their faces, a symbol of penance and mourning. This practice, a sign of mourning, was intended to help a person grow closer to God.

Giving money to the poor. Praying. Fasting. All three activities are some of the most spiritual activities a person can do. So what about Jesus' harsh words? Actually, he is not speaking against these *practices*. He is attacking the way in which they are *being practiced*. He is not concerned about the *method* but the *motive*. As we have seen, Jesus starts with the world's standard of rightness (not murdering, not lying under oath) and then peels off the veneer to see if the heart is good. The same is true here. He takes three righteous and holy actions and shows how the condition of a person's heart determines whether the discipline is a blessing or a hindrance.

Jesus is a genius when it comes to how our hearts work. He exposes people who practice these disciplines in order to impress. They do what they do "to be seen," to gain the respect and the praise of others.

If they wanted to impress others, then Jesus says, "truly they have received their reward." The Greek word for "reward" is in the singular, indicating that it is a one-time reward. They got what they wanted. But God has nothing to do with any of this because he is not in the mind of the person caught up in vainglory. He or she wanted the praise of other people, not intimacy with God.

Relieving the burden of the poor through giving, or earnestly seeking communion with God through prayer, or cleansing and training the body through fasting was not their aim. They were driven by the need to impress others. But how do we know whether someone is driven by vainglory or earnestly seeking to do good?

IGNORANT HANDS, SECRET PLACES, HAPPY FACES

What is the solution to vainglory? Jesus' direction to his followers is not so much about how they are to give alms, pray and fast, but with what intention they should do these things. It is important to note that Jesus does not say, "*If* you fast," but "*When* you fast," indicating he expected his apprentices to do these things. The point is not about the disciplines themselves but about the condition of our heart when we do them.

First, when we give alms we are not to let our left hand know what our right hand is doing. Some scholars believe that Jesus might be referring to the offering box that was on the right side of the entrance to the temple, which meant that the offering was placed with the right hand. This image suggests that we should do this good deed (giving some of our hard-earned money to others) with such unawareness that our left hand doesn't know what our right hand just did. If someone were to ask us later, "Hey, did you give money to the poor a moment ago?" you would answer, "Hmm. Did I? I can't remember," and actually mean it.

Second, in terms of prayer, Jesus encourages us to shut the door to our room and pray to our Father who "is in secret; and your Father who sees in secret will reward you." This is an example of great wordplay. These examples are about people wanting to be seen, but God is unseen. God not only sees in secret but lives in secret. In other words, God is not a God of vainglory. R. T. France notes, "[God] is himself invisible, in contrast to his pretended worshippers, who are only too visible."

Prayer is something deeply personal and private. The "room" Jesus mentions probably is a storage room, because it was the only room that had a lock on it. We should lock the door to be certain that no one sees us praying. That kind of secrecy would ensure that we will not "be seen" by others but will be in close fellowship with God. John Chrysostom wrote, Why "must we pray? Not to instruct Him, but to prevail with Him; to be made intimate with Him, by continuance in supplication; to be humbled; to be reminded of your sins." He says this kind of prayer can only be done "in secret."

Third, Jesus teaches us that fasting should be done without fanfare. When we fast we are not to put on our penitent clothes and smear ash on our faces so that everyone will know we are fasting. Our appearance should be normal. Washing one's face and putting on oil was the normal routine in Jesus' day. Alerting others to the fact that we are fasting reveals our intention to impress people, not to discipline ourselves or heighten our intimacy with God.

HUMILITY: THE OPPOSITE OF VAINGLORY

Jesus encourages us to do good things with absolutely no concern about what others think about us. This is humility, the antithesis of vainglory. The best example of the difference is Jesus' parable of the Pharisee and the tax collector who went to the temple to pray:

The Pharisee, standing by himself, was praying thus, "God, I thank you that I am not like other people: thieves, rogues, adulterers, or even like this tax collector. I fast twice a week; I give a tenth of all my income." But the tax collector, standing far off, would not even look up to heaven, but was beating his breast and saying, "God, be merciful to me, a sinner!" I tell you, this man went down to his home justified rather than the other; for all who exalt themselves will be humbled, but all who humble themselves will be exalted. (Luke 18:11-14)

The Pharisee is a perfect example of vainglory. He loudly lists his accomplishments for all to hear. In contrast, the tax collector beats his breast, confesses his sinfulness and asks for mercy. Humility does not require us to beat our breast and announce our sinfulness. But in this case the tax collector gives us ample evidence of his humility.

Jesus is the prime example of humility. The King of kings and Lord of lords is born a helpless infant to a poor family, lives for a time as a refugee and grows up in a forgotten town. He is baptized by his cousin, then gathers a group of uneducated and unimportant tradesmen, and moving from village to village he dines with known sinners and outcasts. The Son of God became a man without reputation, trading in power for powerlessness and ultimately accepting an unjust death with grace and dignity. As Henri Nouwen notes, "The whole life of Jesus of Nazareth was a life in which all upward mobility was resisted."

THE CURE FOR VAINGLORY

The kingdom narratives oppose the world's narratives: You are valuable to God. God loves you no matter what. Your worth is not dependent on your performance or on what others think of you. Your worth is found in the loving eyes of God. If you win, God loves you. If you lose, God loves you. If you fast and pray and give your money to the poor, God loves you. If you are sinful and selfish, God loves you. He is a covenant God, and his love never changes. You are valuable, precious and worth dying for—just as you are."

Paul says it beautifully: "Not that we are competent of ourselves to claim anything as coming from us; our competence is from God" (2 Corinthians 3:5). We do not need others to affirm us. Our worth comes not from the opinions of others but from God's opinion: we are precious and priceless.

"Live for an audience of One." This Puritan saying perfectly reflects kingdom living. Most of us

---

Have you felt the beginnings of the kingdom core narratives entering your heart? If so, how is that changing your behavior?

---

spend our lives playing for an audience of many, fixating on what others are thinking or saying about us. Seldom do we apply this kind of concern when it comes to God. When we set our minds and hearts on things above (Colossians 3:1), we shift from an audience of many to the audience of One. What we do for God is what really matters.

John Calvin describes how focusing on God leads to a true sense of who we are: "It is evident that man never attains to a true self-knowledge until he has previously contemplated the face of God, and come down after such contemplation to look into himself." True self-knowledge comes from looking into the face of Jesus, not the faces of others.

This doesn't mean we pay no attention to what others say about us, and it certainly doesn't mean we are to disregard good counsel. But we turn our thoughts Godward and always act with God in mind. Then we are free to listen to the appraisals of others—with great discernment. We listen to the opinions of others, but we are not controlled by them.

The kingdom of God is the only place we find real peace. As Augustine said, "Our hearts are restless, O God, until they find their rest in you." No matter how many worldly "trophies" we acquire, we won't be able to lay our head down in peace because we are only as good as our last success. But our loving Father—the only One who matters—tells us that we are loved, that we are of immeasurable worth.

When the kingdom narratives replace the false narratives, we are able to play without needing to win, love without needing to receive, pray without feeling pious and serve without needing to be thanked. Our value is set; our worth is stable and unchanging. We are loved and valuable, no matter what people tell us. When that narrative penetrates our hearts, we become free people indeed. The prayer attributed to St. Francis reflects a kingdom heart:

> O divine Master, grant that I might seek
> not so much to be consoled, as to console;
> to be understood, as to understand;
> and not so much to be loved, as to love another.

Such people are "more than enough" people (see p. 129). They live from the strong foundation of the kingdom and are not as interested in being consoled, understood or loved by people because they already are by God. Instead, they console, understand and love others. Paradoxically, people who learn to do this are the happiest of all people.

THREE THINGS I AM STILL LEARNING

Three things happened since I spoke at the university chapel that continue to instruct me. First, a few months after I returned home I got a letter from a student that shared some of the deep pain he had been experiencing, even wrestling with dark thoughts and bad dreams, during the months leading up to my visit. He shared that somehow God used my talks in chapel to heal his heart, that somehow the Spirit had impressed deeply into his soul that he was valuable, loved unconditionally and meant for something great. This taught me that God can work through a person whose heart has a measure of vainglory.

Second, two years after my talk someone informed me that my talks made the "Chapel Archives," a sort of "Top 30" of the best talks given, on the university's website. I was pleased, which reminded me that vainglory is not fully behind me.

Third, despite the standing ovation and the "greatest chapel hits" inclusion, I have never been asked back to that college. Unfortunately, I still seem to care. A part of me would like to go back just to see if my heart has changed, to see if I could stand in that pulpit with no other purpose than to point students to the good and beautiful God. Nevertheless, I know that the kingdom is not about me but about Jesus. My value is not established by an invitation to speak but by who I am (indwelt by Christ) and where I am (the kingdom of God). As long as I keep those truths in focus, vainglory loses its grip on me.

secret service

The exercise this week is to do five things that will lift someone else's burden. Any act of service that lightens someone's load will do. Examples include doing someone's laundry, filling someone's car with gas, cleaning someone's room, helping put up wallpaper, driving someone to where he or she needs to go, or helping someone complete some tasks.

Other examples:

- Listen, really listen, to someone.

- Offer to serve dinner at a homeless shelter.

- Help your kids with homework.

- Borrow a car over the lunch hour and clean it inside and out.

- Ask God to send you a person in need. Watch out for this one!

Go out and "give me five" this week, five intentional acts of kindness and sensible acts of beauty! However, there is another catch to this one: *You must strive to do it in secret!*

We want to have our good deeds noticed. This can ruin our acts of kindness or generosity, because our motive may be to be rewarded for what we have done. As far as you are able, try to be of service to others without them knowing. It may be impossible to hide it—and don't lie if they ask you about it. Just try not to draw attention to what you have done. It is likely that some of your acts of service will eventually be known. When this happens, simply say, "I just wanted to help you out. It was no big deal," and move on.

One final caution: don't give people money. Certainly there is a place for this, but for now your acts of service should involve your time and energy, not merely writing a check. Keep your acts of service on the nonmonetary level. Experience the joy of putting the needs of others before your own, and break the grip of vainglory in your heart.

nine

Learning to Live
without Avarice

When I was in the fifth grade I saw an advertisement for the most amazing pair of athletic shoes. They were called Adidas Americana and were white with red and blue stripes. Everything about them was cool. In the commercial, the shoes seemed to sparkle as one of my favorite athletes wore them, jumping in slow motion across endless space.

Though I didn't know why, I simply had to have those shoes. I felt a strong emotional need to have them. Unfortunately, they were out of the price range my parents would normally spend on sneakers, which I either wore out or grew out of in a few months. I offered to do extra chores, and they said if I showed interest down the road they would consider it. I never lost my zeal for the Adidases. After a few weeks my father took me to the sacred athletic shoe store, and I bought them. I took them home and adored them. Though I wore them outside to go shoot baskets, I was careful to keep them clean.

For several weeks I cleaned them every night and placed them back in their original box, nestled inside the tissue paper they came with. I treasured those shoes even though they weren't very comfortable or light. I don't think they made me any better or faster when I wore them. But I continued to love and care for them for several months. After a while they got dirty and began to show wear, so I no longer put them in their box at night. I tossed them into the closet along with my other, less sacred shoes.

Eventually, the holes in the shoes became so large that one of my toes began to stick out, so I threw them in the trash. I still remember the day I dumped them. How did something so valuable become worthless? I thought about all of the time I spent caring for them and how much I had emotionally invested in them. And now they sat next to a discarded milk carton in the garbage can. It seemed a little odd, this fall from grace, but I had no desire to retrieve them.

FALSE NARRATIVE: THINGS BRING HAPPINESS

Why did I want those shoes so badly? What was driving me to possess them? I did not know at the time, but I have a pretty good idea now. It wasn't the shoes I wanted so much as what they represented, what owning them would do for me. It is estimated that "roughly ninety percent of our consumer buying behavior is unconscious." We purchase things not merely for their functionality but for what they say about us and what we think they will do for us.

The false narrative that drives our materialism goes something like this: _____ [insert a dollar amount or a material possession] will make me feel secure, powerful, successful and happy.

Notice several things are promised here: security, power, successfulness and happiness. You may object, "C'mon, Jim, the toilet paper I bought last week had nothing to do with security or power or happiness." Maybe not. When it comes to the staples of life (socks, milk, shampoo) we may not be affected much by this false narrative. On the other hand, which toilet paper did you buy? At what store? At what price? Did you get a good discount? And which shampoo did you choose? The one that has the ad that shows men flocking to see the shiny, bouncy beautiful hair of the woman who uses that brand? And did you buy the deodorant whose ad features a man being mauled by beautiful women because he uses that deodorant?

Most of us don't buy things for sheer survival but because of the promise they bring to us. We buy home alarms and antibacterial soap because advertisers convince us we are at great risk without them. We buy designer clothing, sheets and certain automobiles because they communicate success. We believe that nearly everything we buy will make us happy and successful.

And in some ways, we are right. Those sneakers did make me happy. My face lit up when I opened the box each morning. Every time I thought about my new shoes my spirit lifted and a smile came over my face. But it wasn't the leather and rubber and the dye that lifted my spirit. It was what the shoes stood for, what they supposedly did for me. The shoes, carried a mystique with them, a carefully crafted narrative that played on all of my unconscious desires.

They were made by Adidas, a company brand that communicated athletic greatness, quality and coolness. In the ads the shoes glowed, almost divine, as if from another world. My favorite athlete jumped higher than is humanly possible with them on. By owning these shoes I too would be great and certainly cool, and I would become just like my idol, able to jump higher and longer than ever before. I had no idea this was going on in my mind. I just wanted the shoes more than I wanted anything, and I worked and waited to get them. And when I got them, it felt really good.

For a while.

DEEPLY IMPRESSED NARRATIVES

Our minds are like wax imprinted with narratives. This imprinting begins very early and continues throughout our lives. Particularly strong experiences press narratives most deeply into our minds. *Particularly strong* experiences are accompanied by very high and pleasurable or very low and painful events. My sneakers experience was high and pleasurable. It reinforced the false narrative that material stuff can make us happy. I have wrestled with this narrative through-out my life. This narrative, which I adopted early, became a way to understand the world. Those shoes were not the last thing I have purchased based on the false narrative.

The way we way we make purchases and handle our money and material possessions can be traced to our early (often childhood) experiences regarding material wealth. Suze Orman, the popular financial expert, says that when she was a little girl her father's business caught fire, and she re-members vividly her father dash-ing inside the burning building,

> Identify some events in your life that established your narratives in the area of money and wealth.

grabbing the hot metal cash register with his bare hands and run-ning out. He fell to the ground, writhing in pain with scorched and seared hands.

That moment changed her forever, she said. She was too small to process it all, but a narrative emerged: money is very valuable, worth endangering your life by rushing into a building to save; therefore, you must never be careless about money. She credits that moment as making her into a "saver," a diligent money manager: "From that point on, earning money, lots of money, not only became what drove me professionally, but also became my emotional priority."

Suze Orman's narrative became dominant through a painful event. My narrative became dominant through a positive event. When I got those shoes, a rush of dopamine (the pleasure chemical) entered my brain. It felt good. And for several weeks those shoes made me happy. The narrative became deeply ingrained: buying cool stuff is really fun! Even though the feeling wore off, the narrative remained. It was a part of my body and soul.

Most of our narratives develop unconsciously. Striking events or critical moments, like watching Dad sear his hands on a burning cash register, create strong narratives about the value of money and material things. The essence of this false narrative—whether we are a saver or a spender—is similar to others we have looked at: "You are all alone—so either save like a miser or spend like the prodigal." It is fueled by fear, either that we are not valuable without possessions or that we need to save all we can to protect our future.

UNDERSTANDING AVARICE

Just as *vainglory* perfectly describes the need to impress people, *avarice* describes another vice Jesus addresses in the Sermon on the Mount. Avarice is an excessive desire for money or material possessions. It is slightly different that greed. We can be greedy about a lot of things: attention, food, pleasure. Greed desires more of something than is needed. Avarice describes greed for money and possessions. Surprisingly, both the stingy and the spendthrift are in the grip of avarice. Though they appear to be opposites, they share the same belief: money (spent or saved) is what makes a person happy.

Avarice, like *epithumia* and vainglory, is insatiable. Once it takes root, we always want more. Apparently John D. Rockefeller, the wealthiest man in the world, told a reporter that he was not really happy or satisfied. The reporter asked him how much money it would take to make him happy, and Rockefeller said famously, "Just a little bit more." This is true because our fears always outrun our money. And remember, the false narrative is based on that classic fear: I am all alone. Outside of the kingdom of God we are on our own, and we must trust in our resources.

Feeling alone and scared, avarice whispers to us, "Money will make you happy and secure. It will impress others. It will give you power." As always, this is partially true. Having money in the bank does bring a sense of security. Having enough money to pay our bills and enjoy life (vacations, sufficient material needs) does bring us a sense of comfort. And having a really nice _____ *[pair of shoes, car, house, gourmet meal]* does bring a sense of pleasure.

So the narrative "money will make me happy" is *partially* true. We all know that wonderful feeling that comes over us when we buy or are given something truly special. When I ask people about their favorite Christmas gift, they usually light up as they remember some wonderful present; the joy is evident in their faces. How about the feeling we got when we bought our first car? Freedom! Fun! Material things bring a sense of happiness and joy.

But not long after, we lose the elation that we first felt. The toy sits in the corner, the car is not as good as the one we now covet, and the house is just a place to live in—not as nice as our neighbor's, which leads to covetousness. Many of today's purchases are tomorrow's load to the dump. We buy the lie that money and possessions will make us secure and happy, but *eventually* they let us down. Outside the kingdom of God, money and possessions are about all we can turn to in order to have these needs met. Fortunately, we don't have to live outside.

JESUS' NARRATIVES: TREASURES, EYES AND MASTERS

Kingdom economics contrast with worldly economics. Jesus uses three metaphors—two treasures, two eyes and two masters—to describe kingdom economics, which he contrasts with false narratives we find in the world.

1. Two kinds of treasures.

> Do not store up for yourselves treasures on earth, where moth and rust consume and where thieves break in and steal, but store up for yourselves treasures in heaven, where neither moth nor rust consumes and where thieves do not break in and steal. For where your treasure is, there your heart will be also. (Matthew 6:19-21)

Jesus teaches us that there are two kinds of treasures: *earthly* and *heavenly*. Treasures on earth comprise things like money and material possessions. Anything that a thief could steal from us, a moth could nibble on or rust can corrode is an earthly treasure. They are temporary. My Adidas shoes were earthly treasures. Moths didn't eat them, but wear and tear got the best of them. Treasures in heaven relate to the things God is doing. And we know that God is helping people. Thus the best way to lay up treasures in heaven is to live out Matthew 6:33: "Seek ye first the kingdom of God, and his righteousness, and all these things shall be added unto you" (KJV). Seeking the kingdom first will lead us to loving (and thus helping) others.

What exactly is a "treasure"? Dallas Willard explains, "We reveal what our treasures are by what we try to protect, secure, keep." Humans are designed to treasure things. Jesus isn't telling us to *not* treasure things, he is telling us which kinds of things to treasure. We shouldn't treasure a car because it will not be around forever and cannot love back. Treasuring our spouse or friend is a very good investment. He or she is an eternal spiritual being who can return love and can bless the world.

We can invest our time, resources and emotional energy in earthly treasures, or we can lay up treasures in heaven. Most of us do a little of both, I suspect. Jesus is helping us to get our priorities straight. We make a lot of choices each day on the basis of the narratives we embrace. When we adopt Jesus' narrative—which allows possessions without being possessed by them—we can make better use of the precious resources we've been given.

Treasures in heaven are not gained by meritorious acts, "but by belonging to and living by the priorities of the kingdom of heaven." Some people have misinterpreted Jesus' words as encouraging us to increase our good works so we will have a nice house in heaven. That is far from the truth. Our good works do not merit anything except the intrinsic value of growing closer to God and helping put on the character of Christ.

2. Two kinds of eyes.

> The eye is the lamp of the body. So, if your eye is healthy, your
> whole body will be full of light; but if your eye is unhealthy,
> your whole body will be full of darkness. If then the light in you
> is darkness, how great is the darkness! (Matthew 6:22-23)

In this passage Jesus is using cultural idioms (common illustrations) that make little sense to us today. In Jesus day "unhealthy eye"
referred to a stingy, envious, jealous person. A person with a healthy
(clear) eye was generous. Today Jesus might have used a different
metaphor: "If you're tight-fisted, your soul begins to shrivel; if you
have an open hand, your soul will be vibrant." Jesus' point is that
through kingdom economics, his apprentices can be generous with
their money and possessions. Generosity indicates that one is living
in the kingdom.

3. Two kinds of treasures.

> No one can serve two masters; for either he will hate the one and
> love the other, or he will be devoted to the one and despise the
> other. You cannot serve God and mammon. (Matthew 6:24 RSV)

In the final illustration, Jesus points out the logical—but not obvious—truth that we cannot pursue earthly treasures *and* the kingdom of God at the same time.
Mammon refers to wealth or the
spirit of wealth. Jesus says mammon is a rival god. Scholars have
no record of *mammon* being used

> Explain how you previously
> understood this passage.

in a negative way in Hebrew culture, thus Jesus' words must have
shocked his hearers, who typically believed wealth was a sign of
God's blessing. Why was Jesus so bold as to call wealth a god?
Money and wealth are godlike in several ways. First, money out-
lives us, having an almost eternal dimension. Second, it has a wide

circle of influence—everyone respects it. People may not like the rich, but most people respect their money: "Money talks and people listen." Third, wealth pretends to offer what we want from God—security, comfort and happiness. This is why we are prone to "serve" money. But money, wealth and material possessions are not the real issue; our hearts are. It's possible to be very poor and serve mammon; it's possible to be wealthy and have a kingdom heart. The outward issue (money or lack thereof) is not important. The inward issue—where our heart is set—is what really matters. Jesus contrasts God and mammon because they compete for our hearts.

It is impossible to serve God *and* mammon because they have opposite agendas. God wants us to reject mammon and to love and trust him, which is the path to peace and happiness. Mammon wants us to deny God and slavishly pursue happiness through wealth. We cannot move east *and* west at the same time; neither can we look up *and* down at the same time. In the same way, we cannot simultaneously serve God *and* mammon. They are opposites.

There are two types of treasures we can invest in (heavenly or earthly), two kinds of eyes (generous or stingy) and two deities we can serve (God or mammon). Earthly treasures are temporal; heavenly treasures are eternal. The wise choice is obvious. Stingy people are inwardly focused and don't experience joy; generous people are outwardly focused, give freely and experience joy. Giving is the wise choice. Finally, mammon says it can produce peace and happiness, but it fails. God promises peace and happiness, and always delivers. Who will we give our allegiance to? Our loving, giving, endlessly able Father. Jesus is not trying to shame us but is offering good investment advice. And that is because he understands the nature of the kingdom of God.

THE CURE FOR AVARICE

Jesus understood how the kingdom of God operates. The kingdom runs on specific economic principles that contrast with the kingdom

of this world. Our kingdom narrative is *God will provide for and protect me and mine, and therefore I am free to seek his kingdom and invest
the resources he gives me in his endeavors.* The kingdom gives a new
perspective on money. God is out for our good and has endless resources. We can never out ask God.

How does God provide for our needs? Not by dropping money from
the sky or secretly depositing it into our bank account. God moves
money and resources through people. Always. Kingdom economics
works this way. And when God uses money through people, he also
gives it back to them. This is another key to kingdom economics.
Money given on kingdom principles is never lost. Once I loaned $300
for car repairs to a Christian man I hardly knew. He was in need, and
I had the resources to help him. He promised to pay me back, but
never did. After three years I asked a friend, "Do you think I should
call him and ask for the money he owes me?" My friend asked, "Have
you missed that money, Jim?" I answered no. This taught me that God
moves money through us to help others; and when given wisely and
with discernment, that money is never lost. I did not lose $300. No, I
gave it. And God saw to it that I never missed it.

As I reflected on my friends' great question, I remembered a time
during those three years when we were about to come up short due
to unexpected medical bills for our daughter. We needed $500 to pay
our bills. The very day I discovered the shortfall, we got an anony-
mous letter from someone, which said, "I was praying for you all, and
thought this might come in handy." The letter contained a check for
$500. I never even had a chance to worry! When God uses our money,
he also replaces it. This is kingdom economics.

Let me repeat—because there is such bad teaching on this
issue—this is not an investment scheme. I have heard late-night
preachers say, "If you send my ministry a thousand dollars, you
will receive ten thousand dollars in return." Then a couple tells a
story of giving their last penny to the ministry and they miracu-
lously got rich. This is contrary to the rest of Jesus' teaching on

money. Those who give this way—in an attempt to get a lot of money in return—are gripped by avarice, the very thing we are trying to be free of. It is a shame that in the name of Jesus these ministries play on people's fears and desires, take their hard-earned money, and often use it for their own gain.

Once you understand kingdom economics you can better understand Jesus' teaching. Earthly treasures decay. Heavenly treasures (investing in what God is doing) accrue eternal interest. Stingy people do not understand kingdom economics and are afraid to give generously because they fear it will be lost. And mammon is not the right god to serve; mammon makes no return on investments but merely takes from us and enslaves us. God liberates us from the bondage that comes when we love money more than people. Instead of concern for return on investment, apprentices are concerned about "return for the kingdom" (my friend Trevor, a Christian man who works in the business world, coined this phrase). When we invest in what God is doing, there is a return for the advancement of the kingdom. Shoes, cars and stocks cannot make this guarantee.

However, these kingdom economics are a challenge to put it into practice. Mammon's tentacles reach everywhere and will subtly pull us toward itself.

RELIGION AND RETAIL, GOD AND MAMMON

Recently, neurologists scanned the brains of people of faith as they recalled and reexperienced the times they felt close to God, either in prayer, worship or solitude. Then they exposed the same people to stained glass, the smell of incense, icons and other religious images that connected people to God. The same specific area of the brain (called the *caudate nucleus*) lit up in all of these people when they felt connected to God. The *caudate nucleus* is not a "God spot," just the part of our brain that is activated when we feel connected to the divine.

It gets even more interesting. The neurologists similarly tested an-

> To what extent can you relate to the euphoric effect, much like a religious experience, of buying something special?

other group, but this time exposed them to material possessions. When they showed images of products that were tied to "cool" brands, *the exact same area of the brain lit up.* The neuroscientists discovered that people who bought certain items experienced the same sensations as those who had deep religious experiences.

Martin Lindstrom observes:

> When people viewed images associated with the strong brands—the iPods, the Harley-Davidson, the Ferrari, and others—their brains registered the exact same patterns of activity as they did when they viewed the religious images. Bottom line, there was no discernible difference between the way the subjects' brains reacted to powerful brands and the way they reacted to religious icons and figures.

This is why Jesus called mammon a rival god. It also explains why I wanted those Adidas Americana sneakers so badly.

It is hard to avoid the temptations of mammon in contemporary American culture. Advertisers know how to play on our fears and desires. By the age of sixty we will have seen over two million commercials, which is the equivalent of watching nothing but those ads for eight hours a day, seven days a week, *for six straight years.* While they appeal to desire, more ads are tapping into our fears to get us to buy their products. Lindstrom explains:

> Practically every brand category I can think of plays on fear, either directly or indirectly. We're sold medicines to ward off depression, diet pills and gym memberships to prevent obesity, creams and ointments to quiet fears of aging, and even computer software to ward off the terrors of our hard drive crashing. I predict that in the near future advertising will be based

more and more on fear-driven somatic markers, as advertisers attempt to scare us into believing that *not* buying their product will make us feel less safe, less, happy, less free, and less in control of our lives.

This is why living in the kingdom can be a cure to avarice and a way to say no to mammon. We can face those fears because we know who we are (indwelt by Christ) and where we live (in the strong and stable kingdom of God).

SHOULD APPRENTICES LIVE IN POVERTY?

Jesus told the rich young ruler that in order to inherit eternal life he should give all of his money to the poor and follow Jesus (Luke 18:18-23). Many people have taken this to mean that Jesus expects this of all disciples. I don't believe God wants us to live in poverty or as beggars. He never gave that command to anyone else in the Gospels. I believe God wants us to have *adequate* material provision for ourselves and our families. This includes a place to live, food, clothing, insurance, even money for recreation and vacations. I see no conflict with the kingdom of God and using our money to have a comfortable life. Poverty, if you have ever seen it, is not spiritual. It is closer to evil.

But we need to examine what *adequate* material provision looks like. Before we do, we need some perspective: 92 percent of the world's population can't afford a car. Yet in Western culture a car is not a luxury but is considered part of adequate material provision. How about having a home, medical insurance, a savings account and retirement plan? While most of us believe these too are adequate material provisions, we need to remember that most people on earth live without these things. But we need to ask questions like these and then apply the principles of the kingdom to discern how to answer them.

At the next level, though, questions about what we should have and how much we ought to give become more difficult. To be sure, many of us have more than we need, and much of the world lacks what they need. The longer we live in the kingdom of God, the more we will discover the needs of the world. And in light of kingdom economics we will find ourselves more able to give with a cheerful heart.

THE FREEDOM OF SIMPLICITY AND THE JOY OF CONTENTMENT

The kingdom solution is not financial stinginess or carelessness, but simplicity. Simplicity is an inner attitude that affects what we choose to purchase. According the Richard Foster, simplicity is "an inward reality that results in an outward lifestyle." It must first be an *inward reality*. This involves adopting the right narrative about wealth, knowing that it is a provision from God, but must not be treated as a god. If we don't know this inwardly, our attempts at simplicity will result in legalism. Once we have the inward reality in place, we can make our outward, lifestyle decisions.

Instead of being legalistic about the kind of car or home we should own, the best approach is to ask the following questions with our large purchases (and some small ones).

- Do I really need this?

- Will it bring me kingdom joy (and not merely temporary happiness)?

- How much of the money I would spend on this item can I free up to invest in heavenly treasures?

This is the kingdom way to use our money. I am not interested in making a person feel guilty about having a $3.86 latte, owning a Jaguar or vacationing in the Caribbean. Instead, I am interesting in helping people—under the leading of the Spirit and in light of the kingdom—make informed choices about their resources.

The apostle Paul does not say that money is the root of all evil. He said the *love* of money is the root of all evil. Loving money often traps a person. Paul counseled:

> Of course, there is great gain in godliness combined with contentment; for we brought nothing into the world, so that we can take nothing out of it; but if we have food and clothing, we will be *content* with these. But those who want to be rich fall into temptation and are trapped by many senseless and harmful desires that plunge people into ruin and destruction. For *the love of money* is a root of all kinds of evil, and in their eagerness to be rich some have wandered away from the faith and pierced themselves with many pains. (1 Timothy 6:6-10, italics added)

How would you rate yourself in the area of simplicity?

Paul advocates contentment with adequate provisions. Beyond that we are tempted to serve mammon and not God.

NOT A LAW BUT A WAY OF LIFE

We are continually tempted to create laws: A Christian must give everything to the poor. People who love Jesus don't drive luxury cars. It's sinful for a Christian to wear jewelry when there are poor people. We like to make laws because they provide security, allow us to feel good about ourselves and give us a way to judge others. Though Jesus told the rich young man to give away all of his possessions (Luke 18:22), another passage tells of a woman who poured a very expensive jar of oil on Jesus' feet.

> When the disciples saw it, they were angry. "Why this waste? For this ointment could have been sold for a large sum, and the money given to the poor." But Jesus, aware of this, said to them, "Why do you trouble the woman? She has performed a good service for me." (Matthew 26:8-10)

We are tempted to turn Jesus' teachings into universal laws:

- In every situation, you must turn the other cheek and never strike back, even when you see someone being attacked.

- Always tell the truth, even if it ruins your relationships.

- Never let anyone see you pray; Jesus forbids it!

- Give everything away and live in poverty, as Jesus commanded.

Living in the kingdom requires wisdom. It entails understanding Jesus' teachings not as universal laws (except the Great Commandment, to love God, self and neighbor) but as insights for kingdom living. We need to examine the ways we spend money, how we think about possessions, and see them in light of the kingdom of God.

So would I buy those cool athletic shoes today? Maybe. But the decision-making process would be done through the lens of the life with God I have come to know. But I would not love them or invest my emotional life in them as I did when I was eleven. And I would answer a number of questions before I made the purchase: Do I need them? Do I understand that they won't make me content? Am I spending too much on them and thus less able to invest in the kingdom?

Today, I am less likely to spend God's money (I am his steward) on something that I don't need. But I am not going to say there is no way I would do that. I know better. I am a child of God, living in his abundant kingdom and not under a law.

Deaccumulation

The Lenten season is usually a time when people give *up* things (coffee, chocolate, TV) for several weeks. This week I want you to try giving things *away*. Give five things away that would be of some value to someone else. It can't be junk but must be in good shape—something that will be a blessing to someone else.

If at all possible, give these possessions to someone you know. But be careful; some people aren't comfortable accepting unsolicited gifts—especially used ones! Don't give someone your old clothes or a pair of decent shoes you don't need. Your friend will not want this strange handout and may feel you are being condescending. Instead, I am thinking of situations like this: say you have three guitars and you know someone who wants to learn to play guitar but does not have one. Give one of them away. If you have something nice that you are sure a friend would appreciate, bless them with it.

I did this exercise over Lent one year, giving away one thing for each of the forty days of Lent. I had, for example, a pristine copy of a famous novel, and I knew of a friend who loved this author but did not have the book. So I was able to give it to her, and she was genuinely blessed. On the other hand, I had a very nice and barely worn pair of shoes that I did not need. In that case, I dusted them off and took them to the disabled veterans store. I left knowing that someone would appreciate a very nice pair of shoes, and I took comfort knowing that the veterans somehow profited as well.

Some people doing this exercise have very little money. I have had students who, frankly, had very few possessions. If that is the case, be at peace. You probably have a few small items (CDs, books, DVDs) that you could give away. Others have an opposite problem. They have a storage room full of stuff that they don't need. Their challenge is to sort through these things to find what would be of value to others.

Most people, though, struggle with letting go of things. Some of us feel great attachment to everything we own. You may find it difficult to watch your things go out the door. If this is the case, remind yourself that you live in the kingdom and that the things that really make you happy cannot be bought.

One final caveat: Avoid the temptation buy new things to replace those you have given away!

Your aim is to be five things lighter by next week. Think about how much of a blessing they could be in the hands of the right people. Offer this prayer: "God, help me to get these to people who will be blessed by them." God bless you as you de-accumulate.

ten

Learning to Live
without worry

Our daughter Madeline was born with a chromosomal disorder and several birth defects, and she died just after her second birthday. During the two years of her life I spent an enormous amount of time worrying, much more than at any other time in my life. As parents we are called to care for our children, so it is natural to be concerned about their well-being. I imagine that much of the worrying that goes on in the world is due to parents' concern for their children.

My wife, Meghan, and I worried so much because we felt overwhelmed by something that we thought we were incapable of handling. We had to feed Madeline through a tube in her stomach, take her temperature often and monitor her vital statistics regularly. We made weekly trips to various doctors, hoping someone would tell us they had some breakthrough medication or procedure that would cure her. We always came home disappointed. We tried to remain optimistic, but we silently worried. When Madeline died, we went through various stages of loss. Perhaps the only solace was that we stopped worrying about her.

Our son Jacob is a teenager. He has stepped beyond the boundaries of childhood and is becoming a man. He has earned our trust and is going places without our constant surveillance. Consequently we have a new set of worries: *What will happen to our child? Will he be safe? What if someone hits his car? What if he makes bad choices and suffers bad consequences?* There are so many "what if" situations in life that we become overwhelmed if we dwell on them.

Our daughter Hope is now nine years old, and I worry about her as well. I worry that she will be kidnapped. The thought of it is too awful to bear. But we hear stories about that kind of thing and wonder if some deranged person might be lurking outside her school. And I have other common parental concerns: Will she stay healthy? Will her life be free of suffering? Am I a good enough father? Will she make good choices?

Even without children life is full of worries. I also worry about my loved ones and friends. Aging parents, for example, is a cause for concern. And it seems every few months I hear about someone I know contracting a life-threatening disease, losing a job or experiencing the death of a loved one. The newspaper is full of terrible stories of fires and murders, burglaries and kidnappings. Worry always has been a prevalent human problem, but I sometimes wonder if our culture is the worst when it comes to worry. We are exposed to so many fearful things, it seems nearly impossible not to worry.

A CULTURE OF FEAR

What's the best way to sell newspapers and magazines or to increase the ratings for the evening news? Play on people's fears, but do so under the pretext of responsible journalism. You know how it works: "The little freckle on your arm could be a time bomb—story at 10." Or "Our exclusive report on why drinking too much water could send you to the emergency room." We are hooked in an instant.

The media plays on our fears to boost their ratings and sales. Scott Bader-Saye calls this the "fear for profit" syndrome. Media executives, advertisers and politicians use fear to motivate and manipulate us. Barry Glassner gets even more explicit: "Television news programs survive on scares. On local newscasts, where producers live by the dictum 'if it bleeds, it leads,' drug, crime, and disaster stories make up most of the news portion of the broadcasts." Then Glassner adds: "Between 1990 and 1998, when the nation's murder rate declined by 20 percent, the number of murder stories on network newscasts increased 600 percent."

But we have enough to worry about even if we never read a newspaper or watch the evening news. Will we ever come to a place where we can do what Jesus clearly commanded: "Do not worry" (Matthew 6:25)?

> What can we do to combat the media's influence?

THE DEFINITION OF WORRY

Before we examine the source of worry, I want to distinguish between caution and worry. Despite their similarity, worry is *not the same* as being cautious or careful. We should be concerned about many things: locking doors, managing our money wisely and driving carefully on slippery roads. This is not the same as worry. Worry is what we do after we have planned, prepared and acted properly. When we continue to stew about something, we have crossed into the world of worry.

Worry is *a disproportionate level of concern based on an inappropriate measure of fear.* Concern, caution and care are all acceptable and even necessary, but worry is what happens when we go beyond these and fear what we can't control. Worry leads to anxiety; it is impossible to be anxious

> How would you distinguish between worry and being careful or cautious? Give an example.

without having first worried. When we feel anxious we can be sure that we are no longer being careful; we are worrying.

We need to be concerned about things worth being concerned about. We know, for example, that wearing a seat belt could save our life, and we are wise to do so. It is important to regularly wash our hands, wear sunscreen when in the sun and look both ways before crossing the street. Learning how to avoid legitimate dangers is *not* what Jesus is addressing in the Sermon on the Mount. He is explaining how worry is both futile and opposed to kingdom living. When we cross the line from being responsible to being anxious, we have turned our focus away from God and his providence. We do this because we have bought into the lie that worrying helps us.

FALSE NARRATIVE: WORRYING PREVENTS PAIN

Worry harms our relationship with God, causes physical discomfort and destroys joy. We can do nothing better with worry than without it. So why worry? What makes us do something that adds nothing to our lives and yet takes so much away? A false narrative that says, "If we worry enough about something, we will prevent bad things from happening."

We have some concern and do what we can to take care of the potential problem, and we don't worry about it. Then something goes wrong, and we tell ourself, *If I had been more concerned about that, I could have prevented it from happening.* Then, when we are faced with some other concern, instead of letting go of the situation once we have done what we could, we continue to worry and fret, night and day. Then the worry turns out to be wrong. This ought to make us worry less in the future ("Gee, why did I worry so much about that? What a waste!"), but instead we worry more. Why? Our narcissistic and superstitious minds interpret the events in another way: *My worrying prevented that from happening. Next time I will worry even more to prevent harm.*

It sounds silly, but this narrative is indelibly marked on the souls of many people. Every time we worry and something bad happens anyway, we overlook the incident. These are *counternarratives*, instances where the dominant narrative is challenged. We usually disregard counternarratives, so the old narrative stays in place. And each time we worry and the bad thing doesn't come to pass, the false narrative is reinforced. In time we are convinced that worrying is a helpful strategy that keeps us from harm. Even though we say we want to worry less, we can't imagine living without it. So when

> Do you relate to the narrative that by worrying we can gain some control in our lives?

we encounter Jesus' command, "I tell you, do not worry about your life," it appears he is asking us to let go of the one thing that gives us a feeling of control. And that is exactly what he is doing!

JESUS' NARRATIVE: THINGS NOT TO WORRY ABOUT

After discussing the dangers of avarice (Matthew 6:19-24), Jesus addresses the subject of worry through two illustrations:

> Therefore I tell you, do not worry about your life, what you will eat or what you will drink, or about your body, what you will wear. Is not life more than food, and the body more than clothing? Look at the birds of the air; they neither sow nor reap nor gather into barns, and yet your heavenly Father feeds them. Are you not of more value than they? And can any of you by worrying add a single hour to your span of life? And why do you worry about clothing? Consider the lilies of the field, how they grow; they neither toil nor spin, yet I tell you, even Solomon in all his glory was not clothed like one of these. But if God so clothes the grass of the field, which is alive today and tomorrow is thrown into the oven, will he not much more clothe you— you of little faith? Therefore do not worry, saying, "What will

we eat?" or "What will we drink?" or "What will we wear?" For it is the Gentiles who strive for all these things; and indeed your heavenly Father knows that you need all these things. (Matthew 6:25-32)

Jesus says we are not to worry about *food* and *clothing*. These two things are natural human concerns. I think Jesus uses these because they are primary human life needs.

Many people read Jesus' teaching as if he is saying, "You don't need to worry about having food or clothing—just have faith. God will provide them for you," the implication being that with simple faith God will drop food into our mouth and fill our closet with expensive clothes. But the reality is that many faithful men, women and children starve each day. Jesus is *not* saying that people who are indeed poor and hungry—the kind of people who were listening to this sermon—lack faith and need to trust God more. Telling impoverished people they need to have more faith would be cruel and utterly wrong.

> What was Jesus trying to get us to see when he asked, "Are you not of more value than they?"

So what is Jesus saying?

In previous sections Jesus prefaced his teaching with, "You have heard that it was said . . . but I say to you," indicating that his teaching is opposed to the dominant narratives of his culture. Though he doesn't say this here, his teaching once again turns a common teaching upside down. The rabbis often contrasted the carefree life of animals with the constant burden placed on humans to earn their bread by the sweat of their brow. Jesus uses the examples of the birds to show that while they neither sow nor reap they are provided for. The point: Don't worry. New Testament scholars Dale C. Allison and W. D. Davies believe that "this novel twisting of an old motif may well have been deliberate and intended to catch the hearer off guard."

The same is true with the teaching about flowers. In the Hebrew Bible, when flowers or grass is mentioned, it is to show how fleeting and fragile human life is:

> All people are grass,
>> their constancy is like the flower of the field.
>
> The grass withers, the flower fades,
>> when the breath of the LORD blows upon it;
>> surely the people are grass. (Isaiah 40:6-7)

So when Jesus mentions flowers, they would have expected him to say, "Just as the flowers are here today and gone tomorrow, so shall you be. Your life is brief. Make the most of it." Instead he is teaching, "If God takes such great pains to make a little, insignificant flower beautiful, then how much more will he take care of the people he made in his own image."

We may be tempted to think that Jesus is telling us to trust God to provide our needs without our help. Birds, as we know, are not lazy creatures. They actually work very hard. They do not sit in their nests and wait for God to bring them seeds and berries. They actively seek their sustenance. But they do this without worrying. Jesus' point is clear: you are worth far more than a bird. In Jesus' day several birds could be purchased for a handful of change. But we could never put a value on a person. That is Jesus' point.

Earlier in the Sermon, Jesus taught his disciples to pray, "Give us this day our daily bread." If we turn to God and ask him for our daily provisions, we can trust that he will do so. Jesus is arguing from the lesser to the greater: if the birds, who are not so valuable and neither sow nor reap, are provided for, how much more will my Father provide for you, his precious and priceless ones, who work hard for what you have?

Jesus is asking us a profound question: if God provides for the smallest and most insignificant creatures, don't you think he can provide for you, his most precious and important creatures? It's a logical question that helps us move away from worry and into trust. Worry keeps me focused on my own limited resources. Trust keeps my attention on God's abundant resources. This is why worry cannot exist in the kingdom of God. Worry happens when I am on the throne of my life, when I live in the kingdom of me. But we trust when God is on the throne of our lives and we live in his kingdom. That is why the solution to worrying is to seek first the kingdom.

SEEK FIRST THE KINGDOM

Matthew 6:33 is the key to the entire Sermon on the Mount: "Seek first his kingdom and his righteousness, and all these things will be given to you as well" (NIV). If we understood and applied this verse, every single teaching that has come before and after it would naturally fall into place. This principle—seeking the kingdom first—is the cure for all of the common human struggles we have looked at so far (exclusion, anger, lust, lying, retaliation, vanity and avarice) as well as the problem addressed in chapter eleven: judging others.

What does it mean to seek the kingdom of God first? It means making the reality and the principles of God's kingdom our first and primary concern. It doesn't mean we shouldn't work hard. It doesn't mean we shouldn't care about anything or be responsible stewards of our lives and possessions. We continually look to God and what he is doing in the midst of ordinary life. Seeking the kingdom first means facing our trials and troubles not with anxiety but with trust that God can and will work in them.

There are many things, good things, which will compete for our allegiance. For example: Should we care for the poor? Yes, but first we must seek the kingdom. Should we pray? Yes, but first we must seek the kingdom. Should we fight injustice? Yes, but we must first seek the kingdom. Should we walk in the Spirit? Yes, but we must first seek the kingdom. Should we go to church, read our Bibles and witness? Yes, but we must first seek the kingdom of God.

Sometimes we focus all of our attention on a cause, a discipline or even a commandment of God, which are all essential aspects of being Jesus' apprentices. But the most important thing is to seek first the kingdom of God. Then everything falls into its proper place. I pray, care for the poor, fight injustice and attend church not because my concern is prayer, poverty, justice or worship, but because my primary concern is what God is doing. When I am concerned about God and his kingdom, I will naturally do these things as they are needed. The moment I put any of them ahead of the kingdom of God, they become idols, though they are good things.

This is why Jesus says with such clarity and authority, "Seek first the kingdom of God." The kingdom is never in trouble. Individual churches and ministries come and go; even our very lives are transient. Churches are viable insofar as they are connected to the kingdom. Our lives are strong and vibrant only as they are lived within the principles of the kingdom. Our wins and losses don't define us. Who we are (indwelt by Christ) and where we live (in the kingdom of God) defines our lives.

Worry prevents us from seeking the kingdom, just as serving mammon prevents us from serving God. They are mutually exclusive. As Allison and Davies point out, "Anxiety is foolish and accomplishes nothing except to put God out of the picture." This is why Jesus inserts this key verse in the section about worry. As long as we are worrying, we can't seek first the kingdom of God. As long as we are seeking first the kingdom of God, we can't worry.

The certainty of kingdom provision led Paul to write these encouraging words:

> Do not worry about anything, but in everything by prayer and supplication with thanksgiving let your requests be made known to God. And the peace of God, which surpasses all understanding, will guard your hearts and your minds in Christ Jesus. (Philippians 4:6-7)

He echoes Jesus' words: Do not worry. Instead of worrying, Paul says, we ought to pray. God has instituted prayer as one of his means of caring for us. We are invited to turn our cares into prayers. And when we do, we put the matter into God's hands. This does not take away our responsibility in dealing with our concerns, but it places the concerns in the larger context of the kingdom. It allows God to use the resources of the kingdom to meet our needs. When we do this, Paul says, we discover a peace that surpasses our understanding.

ONE DAY AT A TIME

The final admonition Jesus offers in this section of the Sermon is not to worry about *tomorrow*. "So do not worry about tomorrow, for tomorrow will bring worries of its own. Today's trouble is enough for today" (Matthew 6:34). Jesus knows that we worry about our lives, we worry about having enough, and we worry about how we look. He also knows that we worry about the future and simply states the obvious, but in a comical way, which probably made his audience laugh: "You can't worry about tomorrow today because it is not here! Tomorrow will have enough problems! Let today's problems be enough for today."

Jesus says that the kingdom operates only in the present moment. We can only live in the kingdom today. We can't live in it tomorrow. So worrying about tomorrow is a useless distraction. Just as we count on God today, we can count on him tomorrow. But we aren't in tomorrow, and never will be; we live only in the present, in *today*.

Regarding today's troubles, God is teaching us how to respond to them as they come, one by one. Think of the *I Love Lucy* episode where Lucy is wrapping chocolate candies on an assembly line. At first Lucy does all right, but then the conveyor belt speeds up and soon she is way behind. By adding tomorrow's troubles to today, we double our troubles, which is like speeding up the conveyor belt, and suddenly we lose all margin and cannot keep up. We then suffer from worry sickness.

God is working with me, and his kingdom pace is one day at a time. He has wisely ordered and measured what I can handle. Adding tomorrow's problems to today's is actually impossible, but many of us try to do so anyway. Today is the tomorrow that we worried about yesterday, and it added nothing but misery.

Ultimately, worry is futile. Most of our worries are due to the bad habits we learned while living outside of the kingdom of God, when we trusted in things like money and approval, even though they always disappointed. Jesus encourages us to resist the temptation to worry and concentrate on the fact that God is with us in all that we do, which is the right attitude toward the present and the future. My focus ought to be on the present moment. But when we do think about the future, as kingdom-dwellers we can think with hope, plan with confidence and rely on prayer. We have many past blessings on which to base this confidence.

A PERFECTLY SAFE PLACE

I ask two questions of people going through the apprentice series: Who are you, and where are you? I repeat those questions often because repetition is one of the keys to learning. I am looking for these responses: "I am a child of God, one in whom Christ dwells, and I am living in the unshakable kingdom of God." When a person grasps those two realities, many of the problems that plague him or her begin to diminish. This is certainly true of worry. I think about Paul and the hardships he faced, and how he kept his focus on who and where he was:

> But we have this treasure in clay jars, so that it may be made clear that this extraordinary power belongs to God and does not come from us. We are afflicted in every way, but not crushed; perplexed, but not driven to despair; persecuted, but not in forsaken; struck down, but not destroyed. (2 Corinthians 4:7-9)

The treasure we have is Christ in us, and our mortal bodies are the jars of clay. We are Christ-inhabited people, endowed with power to do all things through Christ who strengthens us.

We live in the unshakable kingdom of God, so that even when we are tested, we never fail. This is why I am confident that our world is perfectly safe. *Safe?* you may be thinking. *Are you kidding? This world is scary and dangerous!* That is true if you are on the throne of your life, living outside of the kingdom of God. Inside the kingdom of God we are in no danger.

No danger? You could get cancer, hit by a bus, lose your job or lose a loved one in a heartbeat. Let me say clearly: none of these things can harm those who live in the kingdom. If we die, we step into glory. If we lose a job, we can learn how to trust God for something better. If we lose a loved one, we can be certain that we will soon enjoy their company, for all eternity. As long as we live in fellowship with our good and beautiful God in his mighty kingdom, we have nothing to fear, not even fear itself. For nothing in life or in death can separate us from the love of God (Romans 8:38-39). When we know this to be true, we can let go of worry and begin living with confidence and joy.

SOUL TRAINING

prayer

In this chapter is a verse in which Paul makes a direct connection between prayer and worry:

> Do not *worry* about anything, but in everything by *prayer and supplication* with thanksgiving let your requests be made known to God. And the peace of God, which surpasses all understanding, will guard your hearts and your minds in Christ Jesus. (Philippians 4:6-7)

Once we have done all we can do in a given situation, we simply turn the matter over to God and thus prevent worry from taking over. For example, C. S. Lewis once said that a person who has weeds in his or her garden should not pray about the weeds but pull them up. But when we face situations we cannot change by direct effort, such as a loved one who is ill or a financial problem that extends beyond our resources, then we turn the matter over to God. Here are some practical guidelines to help you turn your cares into prayers this week:

- Each morning set aside ten to fifteen minutes.
- Think about all of the things you might be anxious about.
- Write them down in your journal or a notebook.
- Ask what you can do to remedy each of these situations.
- Make a note to yourself to do the things you can do.
- Turn everything else over to God.

- Write your request to God, and be specific.

Be very specific in your prayers. Why? *Most of our prayers are so vague that we would not even know if God had answered them.* God can handle your specificity. If God has a better way of answering your prayers or dealing with your problems, you can be sure he will. Let him know what you need and desire. Cast your cares on God. Then wait and see what God does.

Prayer helps us deal with our worries in several ways. First, we realize that the provision of the kingdom of God is available to us in every circumstance, large or small. Second, we see things from God's perspective, which puts our problems and concerns in a new light. I find that the practice of writing my prayers forces me to think about my concerns: are they driven by false narrative or centered on the advancement of the kingdom?

This is why I keep a prayer journal. I turn my cares into prayers on a regular basis, and I colabor with God in composing them. This helps my prayer life become a little less selfish. It is hard to write, "God, give me huge amount of money," or "God, can you make my enemies suffer." In the middle of these sentences I would have to stop and laugh at myself. I may actually hope for those things, but they are not legitimate concerns or needs, and they are certainly not driven by seeking the kingdom first.

Prayer is a totally gratuitous gift. God is not obligated to give us this privilege. God gives us this gift to help us discover how loving and caring he is, and to help us grow and mature, which is evidenced by what we ask for. The deeper my heart is in the kingdom of God, the more my prayer life is focused on the well-being of others. This doesn't mean we shouldn't pray for our own needs, but even prayers for our own well-being will reflect the values of the kingdom more than the values of this world.

May you experience the present strength and power of God as you pray, and may your worries diminish with each prayer.

eleven

Learning to Live without Judging others

One day my friend Mark and I met to discuss a matter he said was weighing on his mind.

"I have a close friend who claims to be a Christian but is not living like it," Mark said.

"How so?" I asked.

"Well, he treats his girlfriend badly. He neglects her and is sometimes mean to her. I have witnessed it on several occasions. He often does what he wants to do and almost never does what she wants to do. They are very serious, and he told me he is going to ask her to marry him this summer. It really concerns me, and I have been planning on confronting him about it. There are two ways I am planning on doing it and I want your advice on which is the best way," he said.

"What are the two ways?" I wondered.

"The first is to go to his house and confront him one-on-one. I have written a list of all of the times I have seen him be unkind to his girlfriend, and I am planning on presenting it to him. The second

way is to bring a friend with me who has also witnessed his bad behavior. I remember somewhere in the Bible it says you need to bring
a witness with you or something like that. Anyway, which approach
do you think would be better?"

"Neither," I said.

"Neither?" he responded. "Why?"

"Let me ask you two questions. First, have you ever been confronted like that or, to be more direct, been judged by someone in a
manner like you are talking about?

"Yes," Mark replied. "One time a guy who was in a Bible study
with me had heard that I liked to go to clubs on the weekends, and
he confronted me about it. He said he questioned my salvation."

Then I asked, "Did that approach actually help you?"

"Not really," Mark blurted. "It just made me feel embarrassed and
then angry. I never went back to that Bible study. And no one even
called me to see how I was doing."

"So," I asked, "when someone used the same approach you are
thinking about using, all it did was hurt you and make you turn
away?"

"Right," he said. Then he paused for a moment before saying, "I
think I see what you are getting at. You don't think this approach will
work, right?"

"Let me start by saying that I think it is great that you care about
your friend and his girlfriend and their future marriage. Your heart
is in the right place. And it sounds like your friend really does need
some help. To answer your question, I don't know if it will create the
result you are wanting or not. But I do think that there is a better way
to help someone, a way that is more in sync with the kingdom of
God. Toward the end of the Sermon on the Mount Jesus explains the
right and the wrong ways to try to correct people. If you want," I said,
"We could look at that passage together. Maybe we can find a better
way to do what you want to do."

Mark agreed. For the next several days we met to discuss the kingdom way of correction. Before we looked at what Jesus taught, I wanted my friend to examine the narratives that drive us to judge and condemn others in the first place.

Once we understand our motives, we can begin to find the best way to be helpful to someone.

> Give an example when you have been on the receiving end of judgment. How helpful was it?

THE DIFFERENCE BETWEEN JUDGING AND ASSESSING

I suspect everyone reading this has been judged or unfairly criticized at least once in life. Most of us know how awful it feels and how seldom it actually produces anything other than hurt and anger. Before digging into the issue of judging others, I want to distinguish betwen *judging* and *assessing* someone's performance or behavior.

Assessing others' behavior is a necessary part of life. Good parents pay attention to their children's behavior and are responsible for correcting it when necessary. As a professor, I have to grade papers and exams, take attendance, and evaluate the students' performances, resulting in a final grade. Assessing, evaluating and even grading someone's performance is not the same as judging.

Judging is making *a negative evaluation of others without standing in solidarity with them.* When we judge others we are criticizing them, but not as a caring friend who wants to help. After we critically assess their behavior or character, we walk away. I don't mind critique, but I certainly dislike judgment. The difference lies in the heart of the assessor. For example, suppose Tom goes to his friend and confesses a temptation in his life and asks for support. The friend says he will stand with Tom and even pray for him. After sharing his struggle in more detail, Tom asks his friend, "Do you think this is a problem in my life?" The friend says, "Yes, I think you do have a problem, but I think you can overcome it, and I will be right by your side." Is the

friend judging Tom? Technically yes, in the sense that the friend said
he thinks Tom has a problem. But this is not an example of judging,
because he is standing in solidarity with Tom.

This is crucial because much of what we call "assessing" or "cri-
tiquing" or "just telling the truth" is actually judging. Correcting
someone can be a healthy, even life-enhancing action. Judging others
never is. In order to understand how we can dispense with judging
others by living in the kingdom of God, we need to first understand
what makes judging others so appealing.

FALSE NARRATIVE

There are two primary reasons we judge others: to fix people or to
make us feel better about ourselves. (These two often occur at the
same time.) Though we may say we have good intentions, when
we judge others we demonstrate that we care more about ourselves than the person we are judging. If we really cared, we would
adopt another approach. Let's take a look at why are so quick to
judge others.

Condemnation engineering. When we see someone who is at fault,
caught in sin or behaving badly, we often turn to the method the
world commonly uses to "fix" people: condemnation engineering. A
verbal assault, we think, will set them straight, and it appears to
work. We reason, *If I give so and so a good talking to, they will shape up.*
It is a very powerful weapon in our arsenal. The people we judge or
condemn often shrivel, get angry or cry when under our judgment.
Once in a while a person makes some changes, which reinforces the
narrative that this method works.

Seeing it work increases our confidence in the power of condemnation as a means of correction, and it has become the primary
method people use all over the world. Parents, educators, coaches
and bosses take this route to fix the people under their authority.
Many people believe it is the only way to help others change.

On the other hand, some people are more timid, or as Christians they don't want to appear critical, so they say nothing. So we have two ways to deal with the negative behavior of others: attack or do nothing.

Though judging works in some cases, it fails more often than not for four reasons.

First, it doesn't flow from a heart of love. The judging person doesn't demonstrate love toward the other. Mother Teresa famously said, "If you judge people, you have no time to love them." This is why people don't tolerate judgment. They instinctively know that they are not being loved. If we dive bomb others with our accusatory words and then pull up and fly on, leaving them all alone, they know they have not been loved.

Second, judging someone, even if we are right, takes a shortcut that bypasses a necessary step. When someone is in error, the first step toward change is for the person to admit or recognize that there is a problem. When we judge others, we are *forcing* them to recognize their errors. Again, this sometimes works (e.g., extreme cases of intervention). But in most human interactions this is not received well. Those being judged feel attacked. And the natural reaction is to become defensive and strike back.

Third, judgment is deconstruction without reconstruction. We tear down the house, but we fail to rebuild it. The people we are judging live as they do for many reasons, and they are at the mercy of many dominant narratives.

Condemnation engineering fails because it doesn't factor in that a key ingredient for change is knowing *how* to change. Change involves adopting new narratives, spiritual disciplines, community and the help of God. The process of change is lengthy and challenging, and will usually involve the help of others.

Fourth, our judgment may be (and often is) wrong. The old saying contains a great truth: "Do not judge another until you have walked a mile in their shoes." Our knowledge of another person's plight is limited. We don't know how they feel, what has happened to them in the past or what struggles they face. I once felt a great deal of contempt for a woman because she said and did things that went against my value system. I kept quiet, but inside I would seethe. I silently rehearsed my diatribe, verbally putting her in her place. I am glad I never did. A few years later I got to know her better and learned about her very painful past and present battle with loneliness and depression. Once I heard her story I realized that my judgment had been wrong.

> Have you ever judged someone or been judged and the judgment was based on a wrong assessment? Explain.

Philo of Alexandria is quoted as saying, "Be kind, for everyone you meet is fighting a great battle." I believe this is true, and by remembering this I am less likely to judge and more likely to feel compassion. Condemnation engineering fails because it doesn't come across as loving, it doesn't allow the person to own the need for change, it doesn't offer help toward change, and it may be entirely inaccurate.

Feeling better about ourselves. The second reason we are prone to judge others is because it makes us feel better about ourselves. If we don't feel good about ourself, one way to feel better is to knock someone else down. When we judge others, we feel superior to them. This explains why gossip feels so good. Gossip allows us to escape into a world where we are superior to those we are gossiping about. Their faults are laid bare, and as we focus on their weaknesses and failures we are spared from admitting our own. In fact, by magnifying their errors we can wholly forget we have any. Gossip tastes really good, and we lick our chops during these sessions, but in the end we discover we are feasting on ourselves. We, not those we are attacking, are diminished by our judgment.

Judging others puts us on the moral high ground and diminishes those we are judging. We don't come across as a fellow struggler but as a superior saint. Judging implies that we are right and others are wrong. This feels good to us. We temporarily forget our own failings as we focus on the faults of others. Whether we do this in front of those we judge or behind their backs, the result is the same: We feel better when we are judging them. This is why judgmental people either feel the worst about themselves or mostly deny their own weaknesses. It is also the secret to learning how to dispense with judging others by living in the kingdom of God.

JESUS' NARRATIVE: THE BOARD OF CONDEMNATION

Jesus offers a completely different narrative about how to help others change. Through a stern warning and a pretty funny joke, he thoroughly rejects judging others:

> Do not judge, so that you may not be judged. For with the judgment you make you will be judged, and the measure you give will be the measure you get. Why do you see the speck in your neighbor's eye, but do not notice the log in your own eye? Or how can you say to your neighbor, "Let me take the speck out of your eye," while the log is in your own eye? You hypocrite, first take the log out of your own eye, and then you will see clearly to take the speck out of your neighbor's eye. (Matthew 7:1-5)

Jesus begins with "Do not judge, so that you may not be judged," which some take to mean that if we judge others, God's grace will be taken away from us. That is not what Jesus is saying. He uses the image of a measuring cup ("the measure you give will be the measure you get") to illustrate his point: don't judge others unless you are prepared to live under that arrangement yourself. God is not mentioned, but rather we will be judged by others with the same scrutiny we use. When we judge someone, that person will likely judge us in return: "Who are you to judge me? You're no saint!" And of course, he or she is right. No

Give an example when this has happened to you—either when you were judging or were judged.

matter how correct our judgment is, we are not innocent.

Jesus' first point is clear: if you judge someone, be prepared to be judged in return. Jesus then makes a humorous observation about judging, namely, the hypocrisy that we display when we judge others. Imagine a woman with a log lodged in her eye offering to help a man to dislodge a tiny speck of sawdust in his eye. Jesus' hearers must have laughed out loud at the absurdity of the situation

Most of the time people interpret the log to mean their own sinfulness, as if Jesus is saying, "Who are you to judge? You are more sinful than your neighbor." But this is not logical. Would Jesus really be teaching us that if we somehow get rid of the sin in our life we would then be in a position to judge another? If the log is simply our own sinfulness, then the solution would be to get rid of our sin so we could judge others more effectively. This would go against the tenor of his teaching. So what is the log?

The log is not our sinfulness but *the act of judging*. Judging others makes it impossible to help them. Even if the intention is good, the method is wrong. Judging is not the way to help someone with a problem. It blinds us from seeing a better way.

OF PIGS AND PEARLS:
WHY CONDEMNATION DOES NOT WORK

I am aware that my interpretation of Matthew 7:1-5, as well as the following three sections, are not in agreement with most people's interpretation. Some have said to me, "I think I agree with your interpretation, but it goes against what I have been taught. Why is there so much misunderstanding?" There are many reasons, but the main one is we are examining an ancient document written in a different language. I believe that all of the passages we are studying in this chapter fall under the category of judging others, but others see them as dealing with separate issues. I may be wrong, but I ask that you open your mind to the possibility of seeing the interrelationship of these teachings.

Many think Matthew 7:6 is disconnected to the previous section on judging: "Do not give what is holy to dogs; and do not throw your pearls before swine, or they will trample them under foot and turn and maul you."

Almost everyone I have ever heard quote this verse uses it to describe a situation where one person is not worthy of another's ideas or opinions. "Don't cast your pearls before swine," people say, meaning, "Don't waste your wisdom and brilliance on some dumb soul who cannot understand it." This interpretation is backed by several New Testament scholars. Despite their arguments, I fully disagree.

Some scholars believe Jesus is saying we must not be too severe, but we must also not be too lax. We need to be discriminating. If they are right, then Matthew 7:6 is diametrically opposed to Matthew 7:1-5. In other words: "Don't judge others. But don't waste your time on some people who are not worthy." I prefer another, even simpler interpretation.

When Jesus says we shouldn't give pearls to pigs, he isn't saying they are unworthy but that *they can't digest pearls*. Pigs won't eat pearls! If a farmer did this for a few consecutive days, the pigs would go hungry and attack the farmer. While they can't eat pearls, they can eat humans!

Just as pigs can't digest pearls, people can't digest being judged or condemned. It does not meet their need; it cannot be digested. Even if our judgment is sound, the approach is wrong. They will receive it just as the pigs received pearls. They will go on the offensive. That is how judgment works. The judging person is not being compassionate and understanding, but condescending. And no one likes that or responds well to it.

Do you agree that condemnation is not digestible? Why?

One moment I wish I could do over is when I hurt my son by judging him. Jacob was thirteen and loved playing baseball. The previous year his coach said he was the team's most effective pitcher, and in the season-ending tournament he hit two home runs. But the next year, for a variety of reasons, he was playing poorly. He made errors in the field, walked batters when he pitched and slumped at the plate. Each game became more and more frustrating. The coach moved him to the bottom of the batting order and this only added to the anxiety.

After a particularly bad game I was really upset because Jacob made an error and just stood there while another player went after the ball. He appeared to have given up, to have quit trying. On the ride home we sat in silence. He asked to stop for ice cream, which we always did, but this time I said no.

"Why?" Jacob asked, "because I played so bad tonight?"

"No," I replied defensively, though he was right.

"Then why?"

"Because you don't deserve it. You are not trying hard enough. You aren't practicing hard enough. Sometimes I think you are just plain lazy. You play video games when you could be hitting off the tee. Let me tell you this, it only gets harder. Maybe you just don't have what it takes to be a ball player." I had just cast my pearls, dropped my bombs, and as a result I broke his spirit with my harsh words of judgment.

I looked over and saw a tear run down his cheek. My heart sank. But I was still angry, so I said nothing. Remember, anger is a secondary emotion; fear was producing the anger—my fear that baseball, something that gave him joy and made me proud, was being threatened. I tried to tell myself that I was doing a good thing by trying to "wake him up" or "light a fire" under him.

Jacob could not digest my pearls of wisdom. They were of no benefit to him. Fortunately, I came to my senses the next day and asked his forgiveness. Unfortunately, a lot of parents fail to repent, and over time their children become bitter. Paul writes, "Fathers, do not provoke your children, or they may lose heart" (Colossians 3:21). No wonder so many children grow up with resentment toward their parents. Many parents are dogmatic, impose unfair restrictions, ridicule things their children take seriously and make insulting references about their friends. It should come as no surprise that our children prefer the company of friends and families where they aren't judged and condemned.

Condemnation engineering is prevalent in many families, which explains why so many people can't tolerate a few minutes at a large family gathering. I have seen this repeatedly at weddings I officiate. One person will not come if so and so does, or will attend only if he or she can be seated far from another family member. Condemnation engineering works just like pearls fed to pigs. It fails and harms human relationships.

DON'T JUDGE; ASK AND PRAY

So far Jesus has given us ample reason not to judge others: First, it provokes anger and retaliatory judgment. Second, like a log in our eye condemnation prevents us from being able to help others. Third, it does not nourish because it's indigestible. If we can dispense with judging others, we will be in a position to help others. Assuming we reach that first crucial step, what is the right way to help someone? The answer comes in the next few verses:

> Ask, and it will be given you; search, and you will find; knock, and the door will be opened for you. For everyone who asks receives, and everyone who searches finds, and for everyone who knocks, the door will be opened. Is there anyone among you who, if your child asks for bread, will give a stone? Or if the child asks for a fish, will give a snake? If you then, who are evil, know how to give good gifts to your children, how much more will your Father in heaven give good things to those who ask him! (Matthew 7:7-11)

Most people read this section as if it were unrelated to the previous verses, as if Jesus suddenly switched topics from judgment to prayer. While it is about prayer, I don't think Jesus has switched subjects. The issue is still about helping others. After he has told us how *not* to help others, he now tells us how to benefit others, which is to begin with prayer.

First we must take the log out of our eye; that is, we refuse to judge or use condemnation engineering. We are not God; our judgment is often inaccurate, which fails to help people. We need to examine ourself, and if there is a board in our eye, we can, with the help of the Spirit and perhaps a fellow apprentice of Jesus, begin to work on it. Then we can ask what we can do to help someone who needs to change something in his or her life. Of course there is, and the best way to help another is found in three words: *ask, seek* and *knock*. Remember, even though Jesus is now talking about prayer, he does so in the context of helping people. Let's look briefly at each word to see how we can help in practical ways.

Ask. The first thing we do when trying to help others is to pray for them. When we pray for someone our hearts shift to the person's well-being; it's impossible not to begin to feel compassion for him or her. Prayer also helps us to accurately assess another's situation. Many times I have prayed for a person and felt a gentle correction from the Spirit. For example, I may assume that a person has a certain weakness, so I assume I need to pray for him or her to overcome it. Quite often the Spirit has led me to consider that a deep wound in the person's life is creating the behavior. When I sense this, my prayer shifts from the behavior to the wound, and I ask the Spirit to begin healing that person, not merely to change his or her behavior.

Prayer is a wonderful gift from God that helps us in at least three ways. First and foremost, we are inviting God into the situation. We are not alone, but are colaboring with God in an effort to help others. Second, we begin to feel more compassion and less criticism. Third, we have the wisdom of God available to us. God can provide guidance and perspectives that we do not have on our own. T. W. Manson explains, "The whole business of judging persons is in God's hands, for He alone knows the secrets of men's hearts." Many times while praying for another I have come to see the situation in a new light. This is why Jesus tells us to begin by asking.

After praying for a person for a while, we may be in a position to ask him or her if we can address the situation we are concerned about. I have found that when I am standing firmly in the kingdom of God and have prayed for people, they are more receptive to listen to what I have to say. The caveat, however, is that this should come only after we have spent a lot of time praying for them.

Seek and knock. Jesus then says we are to seek and knock. These are words of persistence that apply in two ways. First, we are to be persistent in our prayers. Second, we need to communicate to the person that we are standing with him or her. Judging others, remember, is to stand at a distance and lob our grenades. In the kingdom we live in union with one another. My brother's struggle is my struggle as well. So we show our love by continuing to pray for the person and by letting the person know that he or she is not alone. This can be done through sending an encouraging card or e-mail, or by calling the person.

Most of the struggle we and our friends face will not go away overnight. Most problems are not overcome with a single prayer, not because God is not strong enough or our prayers are not good enough, but because change often comes slowly. Jesus is telling us that importunity is often necessary. Our persistent prayer is a sign not of a lack of faith but of our love and commitment. God is really good, Jesus tells us, even better than earthly parents who care for their children. God wants to give us good gifts, and apparently dogged determination and diligence in prayer is the way God works in our lives or the lives of those we care about.

Does this interpretation of ask, seek and knock make sense to you? Explain why.

THE LAST WORD ON JUDGING OTHERS

Jesus ends this section of the Sermon with perhaps his most famous words: "In everything do to others as you would have them do to you; for this is the law and the prophets" (Matthew 7:12), which we call "the Golden Rule."

Most people read the Sermon as a random compilation of Jesus' best sayings, but we have been noting all along the importance of order, and the Golden Rule is another example of the order of Jesus' teaching. The Golden Rule is the grand finale of his discussion of condemnation engineering, and his final word is to treat others as we would like to be treated. This is his most direct attack against judging others, because he is reminding us just how much we dislike being judged ourselves.

When I am faced with a situation where I need to correct someone, I ask myself, *How would I want to be dealt with?* This puts a quick halt to my most natural approach (drive-by judging), because I do not like it when people do that to me. If we followed the Golden Rule we would never judge others. John Wesley once said, "Do not unto another what you would not he should do unto you; and you will never more judge your neighbour. . . . You will never mention even the real fault of an absent person." We would help them, pray for them, ask to help them and stand with them, but we would never judge them.

A NEW WAY, A BETTER APPROACH

I began this chapter with a story about Mark, who asked me to help him decide how to confront his friend's bad behavior. I asked him to get out his Bible, and together we looked at Jesus' teaching on judging others (Matthew 7:1-6), how it provokes anger and nearly always fails to bring genuine change. We then looked at the section on asking, seeking and knocking (Matthew 7:7-11), and I explained that this was *the Jesus way* of helping people we think need to change (Matthew 7:12). Mark had been ready to march in, hand his friend his list of infractions and let the judgment itself do the work of transformation. I convinced him that it would not work, and would likely harm the friendship, perhaps irreparably.

"So what should I do?" he asked.

"Spend one week praying for your friend. Don't pray about the situation or how to fix your friend, just pray for your friend, for his well-being, for his relationship with God," I said.

"OK. Then what?"

"Then we will meet again next week, same time, same restaurant," I responded.

"But," he asked, "what about my list? What about my confrontation?"

"Not yet," I said. "Put your list in a drawer for now. Just spend a week praying for him, and then we will enter the next phase."

A week later we met for lunch, and I could tell Mark was very different. He wasn't agitated; he seemed peaceful. I asked him if he had been praying for his friend, and he said he had. "Praying for him changed everything, Jim," he said. "I feel a lot more compassion for him, and my need to attack him is nearly gone. Still, I feel like I want to address this issue with him. What is the next step?"

"Remember *the Jesus way* we talked about last time?" I asked.

"Right. Ask comes first. I think I know what I need to do."

We met again two weeks later, and he was excited to tell me how well it had gone with his friend. Mark shared with me a story that reinforced my appreciation of Jesus' teaching. He said that he remained in a posture of support with his friend, who opened up about his past. Mark's friend, he learned, had an abusive and distant father. Without any prompting, his friend talked about his fear of repeating his father's pattern. He thanked Mark for letting him open up, and he asked Mark to continue to walk with him in a journey toward change.

"I am so thankful I followed Jesus' approach and not my own," Mark concluded. "If I had given him my list and attacked him, even in a spirit of Christian love, it would have backfired. I never knew about his dad, and now I understand him and his struggle a lot better."

Not every story will end this well. There have been times I have followed Jesus' approach and had no success in working toward change, at least as far as I could tell. Some people are not ready to change. The heart is locked from within. Nevertheless, Jesus' method of helping others is by far the best. Judging others is tempting, but it never succeeds long term. The far better approach is to pray for and stand with those we care about. In short, we treat them as we want to be treated. No other teacher in history can surpass the brilliance of Jesus.

> What do you think about Jesus' method of correction? Does it stand a better chance of working than judgment? Why?

Earlier I mentioned when I cast pearls of judgment on my son, Jacob, and how I wish I had a chance to do that over again. We can't reverse the past, but we can redeem our former mistakes. Though I was frustrated that night, by the time I reached home I took a shower, grabbed a cup of coffee and prayed. During that prayer the Spirit reminded me of the right way to correct someone, and I pondered how I would want to be treated if I were in my son's shoes. The answer began to emerge even before I fell asleep.

I went into Jacob's room, and we sat and talked. I apologized, and he accepted. I then said, "Pal, how are you feeling about this season?" He shared how frustrated and anxious he was. We talked about how that is normal when things are going badly, but then we talked about doing the things that we can do, which is to practice hard. I said to him, "I want you to know that I am with you all the way. Whatever you want me to do, I will do." He told me he wanted me to hit him ground balls, to play catch and to pitch to him so he could work on his hitting. For the next month we spent a lot of time doing drills in the hot summer sun. He slowly came out of his slump and his confidence increased. The game became fun again.

I learned a lot through this event. If we really want to see people change, we have to be willing to come alongside and participate with them, to make sacrifices of our own time and energy. I am so thankful that I have the privilege of prayer and the resources of the kingdom of God. Even if Jacob's problem had not been solved, it still would have been a great blessing. We learned about doing the hard work required of all life's endeavors, and in the process my son and I grew closer. Building your life on the commands of Jesus, though sometimes challenging, is building on a solid foundation.

SOUL TRAINING

A Day without Gossip

Throughout the Apprentice Series we have been working from these basic principles: do what you can, not what you can't; begin where you are, not where you want to be; take small, attainable steps toward change, not impossible steps that lead to failure. With that in mind, this week I would like us to work on an area of our lives that we often tolerate as a kind of "acceptable sin": gossip.

Perhaps the most pervasive form of judgment is gossip. I define gossip as (1) speaking negatively (2) about someone who is not present. Those are the two elements of gossip. If you say something positive ("Brad got a promotion at work; he is such a hard worker"), or if the person is present ("Did you hear about Brad's promotion? Tell them, Brad, or do you want me to?"), it's not gossip.

This week try to go one to three days without gossiping. Forgoing gossip for a single day can be challenging, but try to go for at least three days without saying anything negative about a person who is not present.

John Wesley created small groups of three to five serious apprentices of Jesus, which he called bands. Among the basic rules Wesley drew up for the bands was this: "Not to mention the fault of any behind his back, and to stop short those that do." The first part fits my description of gossip (mentioning the fault of someone not present), but I particularly like the second part (stopping others who are gossiping). I would like you to try that second part as well. When you are in a situation where someone is gossiping, simply interject something like, "Perhaps it's best not to talk about someone who is not present."

This may come off as self-righteous to the gossiping person, especially if that person has known you to gossip. If you feel that something like that is too strong, (1) simply walk away when others are gossiping or (2) refuse to participate and change the subject as soon as you can. I have noticed that restraint inspires restraint. In other words, when we see someone refusing to gossip, it can remind us that gossip is wrong and help us to quit doing it right on the spot. My friend Matt Johnson finds this helpful: before gossip gets out of hand he alters the conversation by saying something positive about the person being attacked: "Well, I don't know Tom as well as you, but he appears to be a really generous person." According to Matt, this reframes the conversation and usually defuses the gossip.

Through the years I have come to see more clearly the destructive nature of gossip. We sometimes condone it because it doesn't feel like a terrible sin. We even rationalize it by calling it other names: evaluation, sharing, discussing a situation. And to be sure, there are times when we are called on to tell the truth about a person not present. For example, I frequently am asked to be a reference for a person, and it is my duty to be honest. When asked if a person is reliable and I have experienced the person as unreliable, I must tell the truth. That is not gossip.

Despite that warning, I believe that most of us know exactly what gossip is and when we or someone else is doing it. Even when I try to spin it as "just being honest about a person," I know in my heart when I am trying to tear someone down. Refusing to gossip and trusting God to help us silence as much gossip as we can is one of the most loving things we can do for others. Again, we begin with what we can do, not what we can't. Progress in the spiritual life works this way. I believe you can live a day without gossip. And when you do, I trust that you will see that you are capable of living without it.

twelve

LIVING IN THE KINGDOM DAY BY DAY

There is something very peaceful about sitting in front of a fire on a snowy day. In fact, as I write these words I am sitting in front of our glowing fireplace while giant snowflakes are falling outside. Sitting by a warm fire is a soul-enriching experience for me. Through the centuries starting and tending a fire has been a helpful metaphor for the spiritual life. Thomas Kelly, the great Quaker professor and author, wrote about "burning the flame of the inner sanctuary" as an image for nurturing our prayer life. Madame Guyon and John Wesley also used the metaphor of a fire to illustrate the collaborative work between God and humans. They spoke of how we must create the conditions and do the preparatory work, but God alone is the spark that ignites the flame in our souls.

For me, the image of building and tending a fire is a perfect illustration of what it has been like to maintain a vibrant life with God. In days gone by the first duty of the father or mother of the house was to get up early and start the fire in the hearth. Throughout the day someone would stoke the fire, adding new logs to keep it burning strong. If it was not tended, the fire would die out. That is exactly how my own devotional life works. In the morning I try to set aside time, a half hour at least, for private prayer. This is how I start the fire each day. Through adoration, thanksgiving, recollection, praise and surrender, I interact with the God who sacrificed himself for me, and surrender myself to his guidance and will.

But that is not the end for me. Just like the fire in the fireplace, I need to stoke the fire throughout the day. I do this by pausing for short times of prayer every hour or two, by reading the Scriptures or spending a few moments reading a devotional book, such as *The Imitation of Christ* by Thomas à Kempis. These are the logs that I add to the existing fire to keep it burning brightly. In the evening, before bed, I read some other Christian book, spend a few moments in self-examination, going over my day with God in prayer and then fall asleep in his tranquil presence. I don't do these things because I want God to love me and bless me, nor to avoid punishment or impress people with my piety. I do all of this to keep the fire burning. *I do them because I am spiritually weak.* I cannot maintain an effective and joyful Christian life without these activities. I also need weekly times of worship, fellowship and a host of other disciplines to nourish my soul. When I neglect these things, my soul atrophies. I simply know of no other way to be an apprentice of Jesus.

TWO FALSE NARRATIVES

1. What matters is having faith in Jesus, not having an ongoing relationship with him. Not long after becoming a new Christian, I came under the mentorship of Richard Foster, a leading teacher and writer in Christian spiritual formation. Richard taught me how to maintain private prayer, devotional reading, studying the Scriptures and the like. He taught me this way of living by his own example and by introducing me to the great devotional masters of the past. I followed their example and experienced an infusion of life and power through the Spirit. I developed a very real and intimate life with God. I was still a fairly new Christian, so I assumed that all Christians live this way.

I was wrong.

I later learned that people who are close to Christ and his kingdom are the exception, not the rule. Some estimate that only 10 percent of Christians are actively developing their relationship with God on a daily basis. Why? There are many reasons, but I believe there is a theological misstep behind this problem. Many Christians have been taught that a relationship with Jesus is not important. Things like private prayer, personal Bible study, solitude, devotional reading and serving others are rarely taught, and thus are seen as add-ons practiced by the most zealous, overachieving Christians.

2. *The only way to be a good Christian is to keep all of the rules.* Another narrative contributes to the problem as well. In some Christian circles the dominant message is that Christian living is a matter of keeping all of the right rules. The focus is on doing or not doing certain practices. But mere rule keeping leads to an unsatisfying Christian life. Our souls hunger for something deeper than a list of dos and don'ts.

Neither false narrative is right. The first sees the spiritual disciplines as unnecessary. The second sees them as mandatory. Both miss the key element: relationship. What truly matters is a relationship with Jesus, with being his apprentice. This naturally entails engaging in practices that nurture the relationship (contra the first narrative). But the relationship is what is important, not the practices themselves (contra the second narrative). Spiritual exercises are wise practices that develop and enhance our life with God, but they are not spiritual merit badges that determine how God feels about us. Apprentices of Jesus learn how to be with Jesus in order to become like Jesus, and that is done by learning how to abide in him.

JESUS' NARRATIVE: ABIDE IN ME AND BEAR FRUIT

The secret to living a vibrant Christian life is abiding in Jesus. There is no other way to wholeness and happiness than to live in utter dependence on Jesus. He used the image of a vine and its branches to describe how his disciples ought to live:

> I am the vine, you are the branches; he who abides in Me and I in him, he bears much fruit, for apart from Me you can do nothing.
>
> If anyone does not abide in Me, he is thrown away as a branch and dries up; and they gather them, and cast them into the fire and they are burned.
>
> If you abide in Me, and My words abide in you, ask whatever you wish, and it will be done for you.
>
> My Father is glorified by this, that you bear much fruit, and so prove to be My disciples.
>
> (John 15:5-8 NASB)

The image of a vine and its branches describes the necessity of staying connected to Jesus. A branch not attached to the vine is cut off from life and energy, and cannot bear fruit, which it is designed to do. In the same way, a Christian who lives apart from Jesus is disconnected from Jesus' life and power, and cannot bear the fruit of the Spirit (love, joy, peace, patience, kindness, goodness, faithfulness, gentleness and self-control).

Most of us would like to live with joy. The majority of people I know would like to be thought of as good people. I know very few people who would not like to have more peace. Jesus says that these things naturally will become a part of our lives and our character if we abide in him. But apart from him we can do nothing; we cannot bear this fruit anymore than a cut branch can bear fruit.

How do we abide in Jesus? What does that look like? In *The Good and Beautiful God* I explained it this way: "to abide means to rest and rely on Jesus, who is not outside of us, judging us, but inside of us, empowering us. The more deeply we are aware of our identity in Christ, and of his presence and power that are with us, the more naturally we will do this." To abide, then, is not done by observing a set of outer activities. I can't nurture my relationship with my wife merely by doing certain activities, such as sending flowers or writing her notes. Those things can be wonderful if my intention is to express my love. But developing the relationship will involve much more—spending time with her, listening to her and caring for her.

How do we abide in Christ? What is your experience of this?

To abide in Christ involves spending time with Jesus. For me, this happens when I keep my mind and my heart set on his presence with me. Psalm 16:8 reads, "I have set the LORD continually before me; Because He is at my right hand, I will not be shaken" (NASB). Colossians 3:1-2 counsels, "Since, then, you have been raised with Christ, set your hearts on things above, where Christ is seated at the right hand of God. Set your minds on things above, not on earthly things" (NIV). My problem is that my mind wanders a great deal. That is precisely why I need to find ways to reset my mind on things above, where Christ is.

The focus should be on the relationship, not the rules. Our Christian lives are in real trouble when we focus mainly on rule keeping. We must remain focused on our identity in Christ and let that determine our behavior. When I know and reflect on the reality that Christ dwells in me, my desire to nurture that relationship strengthens. But I must do something to build that relationship. Thus I have many practices (not rules) that help me develop my relationship with God. Our souls hunger for relationship, which the disciplines nourish.

FOUR IMAGES, ONE POINT

We have arrived at the final section of the Sermon on the Mount, the greatest sermon ever given to the world by the most brilliant person who ever lived. In his clarion call to live as his apprentices, Jesus uses four illustrations that essentially make the same point: arranging your life around Jesus and his teaching is the only way to a good life.

1. There is only one way to the good and beautiful life.

> Enter through the narrow gate; for the gate is wide and the road is easy that leads to destruction, and there are many who take it. For the gate is narrow and the road is hard that leads to life, and there are few who find it. (Matthew 7:13-14)

The first image Jesus uses is of two gates leading to two roads—one narrow and wide. The wide gate leads to the easy way, and the narrow gate to the hard. Taking the path of the wide gate leads to destruction; the path of the narrow gate leads to eternal life.

Jesus clearly says that the narrow way (following his teachings) is challenging, but he also adds that it leads to life. Much is made about the cost of discipleship and how hard it is to follow Jesus. While that is true, it is much harder not to follow him. Why don't we talk about the cost of nondiscipleship? That cost, according to Dallas Willard, is much higher:

> Nondiscipleship costs abiding peace, a life penetrated throughout by love, faith that sees everything in light of God's overriding governance for good, hopefulness that stands firm in the most discouraging circumstances, power to do what is right and withstand the forces of evil. In short, it costs exactly that abundance of life Jesus said he came to bring (John 10:10). The cross-shaped yoke of Christ is after all an instrument of liberation and power to those who live with him in it.

> Why do some people conclude that doing the things Jesus commands is not necessary in order to be a Christian?

Instead of focusing so much on the cost of discipleship, I think we should stress how bankrupt *non-discipleship* is. Jesus knew that many would not practice what he preached and would instead take the seemingly easier road of self-focus. Though it seems easy and is certainly popular, it is the path of ruin.

2. From the inside out. After his teaching on the wide and narrow way, Jesus offers another contrast—inner character versus the outer appearance:

> Beware of false prophets, who come to you in sheep's clothing but inwardly are ravenous wolves. You will know them by their fruits. Are grapes gathered from thorns, or figs from thistles? In the same way, every good tree bears good fruit, but the bad tree bears bad fruit. A good tree cannot bear bad fruit, nor can a bad tree bear good fruit. Every tree that does not bear good fruit is cut down and thrown into the fire. Thus you will know them by their fruits. (Matthew 7:15-20)

Church father John Chrysostom interpreted this passage by saying that the false prophets are not "heretics, but them that are of a corrupt life, yet wear a mask of virtue." He goes on to say that we ought not "look to the mask but to the behavioral fruits of those who patiently pursue the narrow way."

This seems right to me, and it's in the spirit of the Sermon on the Mount. What matters is the inside, in our hearts, as Jesus has said throughout. We may never kill anyone, but we may have a lot of anger in our hearts. Jesus reminds us that his apprentices don't merely look good on the outside but their hearts are being transformed through their relationship to Jesus and the kingdom. When we develop that relationship, we abide in Christ, and we naturally bear good fruit. There is no way to develop the fruit without abiding in Christ. As a teacher, writer and minister, these words remind me that my inner character is more important than my words.

3. There is only one way to the kingdom. Next, Jesus tells us that the only way to enter the kingdom is to "do the will" of his Father in heaven:

> Not everyone who says to me, "Lord, Lord," will enter the king-
> dom of heaven, but only the one who does the will of my Father
> in heaven. On that day many will say to me, "Lord, Lord, did
> we not prophesy in your name, and cast out demons in your
> name, and do many deeds of power in your name?" Then I will
> declare to them, "I never knew you; go away from me, you evil-
> doers." (Matthew 7:21-23)

It is easy to focus here on the phrase "does the will of my Father
in heaven," and turn this section into a call to obey God's will. Obedience to the will of God is central, but as I proposed earlier, for
many that means keeping rules.

The best way to interpret this section is to focus on the four words
I never knew you. Once again, it is about relationship—or lack thereof.
Jesus is pointing out the centrality of a relationship with him, not
merely doing good works. And notice the examples he uses: proph-
esying, casting out demons and deeds of power. He is not merely
talking about attending church or reading the Bible. Jesus gives examples that would make us assume the person was a true Christian.
But Jesus indicates that it is possible to do these powerful works and
yet not be in relationship with him. According to Jesus, that relationship is all that matters.

4. There is only one way to build a good life. We have now arrived
at the end of a careful study of this Sermon and its implications for
our lives. We are also back to where we started. In the opening chapter of this book we looked at Jesus' admonition to build our lives on
the "rock."

> Everyone then who hears these words of mine and acts on them
> will be like a wise man who built his house on rock. The rain
> fell, the floods came, and the winds blew and beat on that
> house, but it did not fall, because it had been founded on rock.
> And everyone who hears these words of mine and does not act
> on them will be like a foolish man who built his house on sand.

The rain fell, and the floods came, and the winds blew and beat against that house, and it fell—and great was its fall! (Matthew 7:24-27)

Everyone in Jesus' day would have been familiar with this illustration. A home's foundation is the anchor that holds the house together through the storms.

But Jesus is not giving a lecture on good home-building practices. He is ending his sermon with a very striking illustration about being or not being his apprentice. Jesus is saying, "There are two ways to live—either as my disciple or not. Being my disciple will mean developing an ongoing, daily relationship with me. Those who follow the principles of the kingdom will be strong and invulnerable. When trials come at you, you will be able to withstand it." For the past three years I have been in community with a group of people who have been "pickling" in the kingdom together. Week after week we study the Sermon and labor to apply it to our lives. We have blessed those who curse us, experimented with ways to eliminate anger and actively sought the kingdom of God in our daily lives. I have seen a lot of great things happen in our lives, but the one thing that has stood out to me is how we have learned to face adversity.

One member of our group, a doctor, was wrongly sued for malpractice. Daily she endured lawyers who were trying to assassinate her character. Though it hurt, and many tears were shed, she stood firm and behaved with a kingdom heart. She was wounded, but she says, "I could not have made it through this several years ago. Before I knew how to live in the kingdom of God I would have been broken by this." As an apprentice of

> Give an example of how not doing what Jesus teaches (truth telling, living without anger, not worrying) has led to harm in your life or someone you know.

Jesus she looks forward to a good future because she is in fellowship with a good and beautiful heavenly Father in a kingdom that has never been and never will be in trouble. A storm came into her life, and the foundation held firm.

SETTING OUR HEARTS AND MINDS ON THINGS ABOVE

How do you keep the fire burning? What are the activities that fuel your spiritual life?

The only way to nurture my relationship with Jesus is to set my heart and mind on the kingdom of God. The fundamental building block of an apprentice of Jesus is living closely to Jesus in our ordinary lives. If we can learn how to spend an ordinary day with our minds set on things above, we will have learned one of the most important spiritual exercises in the Christian life.

To build our lives on the rock of Jesus' teaching, we need to take control of our time, instead of letting time control us. The most fre-

What part of the Sermon on the Mount is most helpful to you?

quent excuse for not growing in our spiritual lives is lack of time. Most of us live at the mercy of our schedule, instead of planning ahead and arranging our schedule around our apprenticeship to Jesus.

SOUL TRAINING

LIVING ONE DAY DEVOTIONALLY

The spiritual tool for this week is perhaps the most transformational of the Apprentice Series. It is one of the main ways I keep the fire burning on a regular basis.

A spiritual discipline I have found particularly helpful comes from Madame Jeanne Guyon (1648-1717), who lived in France and wrote a lot on the spiritual life, her most famous book being the classic *Experiencing the Depths of Jesus Christ*. Madame Guyon suffered a great deal in her life, but she managed to develop a deep relationship with God that brought her great peace.

Madame Guyon wrote a treatise to her daughter concerning how to order her daily life around her faith. She titled it *How to Pass the Day Devotionally*. It is a short and simple yet profound way to pause throughout the day in order to reconnect with God. On pages 216-17 is her account of how to do this. I would like you to consider following her pattern for at least one day this week, and more if possible. I think you will find it encouraging, and you may want to live this way every day. Read through her instructions first, and then I will offer some advice about how you can incorporate some of the Apprentice Series exercises in conjunction with it. I hope you see how this exercise brings together many of the previous practices in the curriculum so far.

"A MOTHER'S ADVICE TO HER DAUGHTER"
by Madame Guyon

How to Pass the Day Devotionally.

1. Go to bed at a reasonable hour. Where there is no set time you cannot establish a pattern. In order not to sleep in too late in the morning, be sure you stay up no later than ten o'clock at night.

2. As soon as you awake, present your first thoughts to the Lord, and offer him the first fruits of the day. As soon as you arise, remember to fall on your knees before God in an act of honor due to his supreme majesty.

3. After you are dressed for the day, spend half an hour in devotion. In that quiet time reflect on the sacrifice that Christ made of himself to the eternal Father, and offer yourself to him, that he may do with you, and in you, what he pleases. Let your principal exercise be an absolute submission to the whole will of God. Remember, to serve him is to reign.

4. Never pass the morning without reading some spiritual book, such as Thomas à Kempis's *The Imitation of Christ*. Do not read too much, but what you do read, read with relish and an aim toward application. Read slowly.

5. And when you come from this time of devotion, be careful not to let your spiritual thoughts fade away, but preserve what you have received as a precious gift you do not want to neglect. The fire kindled in prayer soon goes out if it is not kept up the rest of the day. The fuel you must feed it with is frequent recollection, through prayers of love, thanksgiving

and the offering of yourself to God. As you go through the day turn you mind inwardly, for there you will find God, who is the center of your soul.

6. In addition to times when you pause for prayer, whenever you have free time you must read the Holy Scripture. This will give you guidance as to how to live as a Christian. Read it often. Make it your principal study. Let it be your daily bread. You will learn there, from Christ himself, what you are called to do, and how not to offend him. Therefore, my dear child I advise you not to pass one day without reading at least a portion of the Bible. Sometimes you may read where the book opens, but let your general method be to read it in order, beginning where you left off last, that you may better understand its beauty and relish its sweetness. Read with humility, with an open and searching mind, in order to edify and nourish your soul. Ask yourself as you reflect: Based on this passage of the Bible, what is God calling me to do today?

7. You may pass the rest of your day at work or in visiting your friends. But have this goal in mind: Never spend an entire day without reserving some part of it for recollection and prayer.

8. As you prepare for sleep try to examine yourself, particularly, your thoughts and words and actions of the previous day. Do this with a contrite heart and make a resolution to improve tomorrow and ask God for his assistance. Bask in the peaceful presence of God until you drop asleep. This will make you rest well. Rise again in that same disposition of humility and adoration and surrender, and do the same thing the next day.

HOW TO PRACTICE MADAME GUYON'S METHOD

1. Go to bed at a reasonable hour (say 10 p.m.). Remember, sleep was the very first exercise we engaged in the Apprentice curriculum (in the first book, *The Good and Beautiful God*). We must be rested in order to awake and focus on God. We cannot live an effective life as a Christ-follower if we are exhausted. A good day starts the night before.

2. Turn your thoughts to God as soon as you awake. A key apprentice practice is setting our minds on things above (Colossians 3:1), on having the right narratives and ideas about God. This is a great way to begin your day—turn to God and offer a prayer. You may want to say, "This is a day you have made for me, God, so I will rejoice and be glad in it. Be with me this day, and help me to trust in you for all that I do this day."

3. Spend a half hour in a time of devotion. This may be a challenge for some, depending on your schedule. It will likely mean getting up a half hour earlier than normal—hence the need to "go to bed at a reasonable hour." If you can only find fifteen minutes, that is at least a good start. What will you do during this time? Madame Guyon suggests that we reflect on the sacrifice made by Jesus, and then offer ourselves to God in response. For me, this involves being still for a few minutes and then spending time reflecting on the passion of Jesus. Then I usually pray something like, "As you have given yourself to me, so I will give myself to you, God." Sometimes I pray a famous prayer of John Wesley, known as the "Covenant Prayer."

I am no longer my own but yours.
put me to what you will,
rank me with whom you will;
put me to doing, put me to suffering;
let me be exalted for you or brought low for you;
let me be full, let me be empty;

let me have all things, let me have nothing;

I freely and heartily yield all things to your pleasure and disposal.

And now, glorious and blessed God, Father, Son, and Holy Spirit, you are mine and I am yours.

So be it.

And the Covenant which I have made on earth,

let it be ratified in heaven.

4. Set aside time to read a devotional book. Madame Guyon suggests Thomas à Kempis's *The Imitation of Christ*, which is written in short passages that are full of depth and are perfect for reading in short segments. Whatever devotional you find helpful will do. Many people also enjoy Oswald Chambers's classic *My Utmost for His Highest* or perhaps a daily devotional booklet such as *The Upper Room* or *Guideposts*.

5. Turn to God in prayer throughout the day. I like to pause between activities for a few minutes (five to ten minutes is all I need) to be still and turn my thoughts to God. This is a great way to give your cares and concerns to him. Whatever is on your heart, turn it into a prayer. It may also be helpful to pray the Twenty-third Psalm once each day. This can be done when you are walking or driving.

6. Set aside time to read from the Bible. This does not have to be an in-depth Bible study. I like to have the Scriptures wash over my mind. Currently I am working my way through 1 Corinthians, reading a few verses a day. I like to do this mid-morning, in-between classes. You will need to find a break in your day when you can do this. For some it may have to be before or after a lunch or coffee break.

7. End your day with a time of self-examination and prayer. As you fall asleep, think over the previous day. Ask yourself if there is anything you wish you had not done or had done in another way.

This is what it means to examine yourself. Turn the matter over to God and seek his wisdom, especially if you are unsure about whether something is a sin. If you discover a fault, then resolve to amend your behavior in the future and ask God to assist you. Not all of your behavior will be negative, and in fact, there likely will be things that you did well. Be sure to give thanks and rejoice over those things.

I also like to fall asleep counting my blessings. As the old song goes, "If you're worried and you can't sleep, / just count your blessings instead of sheep, / and you'll fall asleep counting your blessings."

8. One final warning: don't fall into legalism by trying to do it exactly as Madame Guyon prescribes. Focus on the spirit of the exercise; don't turn it into law. And don't conclude that you must do this exercise every day. Remember, the spiritual tools are wise ways to live with God, not means to getting God to like us.

This exercise is a great blessing to me, and if it is for you, I recommend that you do it as often as you can.

appendix

small group discussion guide

by matthew johnson

My first experience with the **Apprentice** Series came when I attended an experimental class being led by James Bryan Smith, which he called the Apprentice class. I **knew** Dr. Smith and the quality of his life and teaching, but I was not prepared for the impact this class would have on my life and ministry. Soon I found myself taking this same teaching into the church where I serve, and the results were no less profound.

Along the way I have found community truly is one of the key components of transformation. This has been lived out by those of us who have worked through this book in small groups—reading, practicing and then discussing what we experienced. The result has been the healing of our narratives, the joy of connecting on a personal level with others, and lives transformed to be more like Jesus. This discussion guide was created out of these experiences to help others develop a similar group of friends, family, youth, Sunday school class or book club.

A group can range in size from two to twelve people. I have found the ideal size is five or six people. With a group of this size, you can easily read through the questions in the guide and share your thoughts and answers. Some groups find that they function well with shared leadership, perhaps rotating the point person from week to week. If the group has twelve or more members, it will work best to appoint one leader.

Each session is split into segments. Use these segments in whatever way is most comfortable for your setting. Feel free to skip questions or segments, and to add questions of your own. In addition, you may want to spend time as a group looking at the questions sprinkled throughout each chapter, discussing anything you found particularly helpful or challenging.

Depending on the size of your group, following these discussion guides could take anywhere from sixty to ninety minutes. I have included estimates on how long each segment will take. If your group has more than six participants, expect the group time to last ninety minutes.

If you are the designated leader of a group that is working through this book, you can use this guide as a starting point, making your own creative changes as you prepare, or you can visit www.apprenticeofjesus.org to explore supplemental materials that give more options for class and discussion experiences. Through the website, leaders can interact with each other and find additional resources.

May God's Spirit work through this guide and lead you deeper into the good and beautiful life.

CHAPTER 1: THE GOOD AND BEAUTIFUL LIFE

OPENING TO GOD [5 MINUTES]

Begin with five minutes of silence followed by a brief prayer inviting God to guide the conversation. *Why 5 minutes of silence?* We live in a busy world filled with noise and distractions. It is easy to enter one conversation still processing the last conversation. In the midst of all this busyness it is also difficult to hear the whispering voice of God. When we gather with friends to share our spiritual journey, we want to hear God's voice in the lives of those around us. With a little silence we will be prepared to listen, so one option is to begin each gathering with some silence.

SOUL TRAINING [15-20 MINUTES]

If you are in a group of six or more people, divide into groups of three or four. Have anyone who is comfortable share either of their two letters. After those who want to share have done so consider these questions:

1. What spoke to you as others in your group shared their letters?

2. What insights did you gain as you wrote your own letter?

3. What did you learn about God or yourself through the exercise?

ENGAGING THE CHAPTER [25-45 MINUTES]

The primary focus of this chapter is that all humans desire happiness, but not all narratives lead to happiness. The narratives of Jesus are the best guide to a good and beautiful life.

[Note: Read through the following questions before you begin discussion. Note any questions you especially want to discuss. Depending on your group size and the conversation, you may not have time to discuss all these questions.]

1. In this chapter we hear the story of Ben (pp. 18-19), a man who lived an ambitious, selfish, even sinful life, but he also found re-

demption and radiance before his life was over. What people have you known who in old age were living the fruit of their narratives (good or bad)? What wisdom can you gain from them?

2. On pages 20-21 the author gives us multiple false narratives about acquiring happiness. Review those paragraphs and discuss the narrative that you see most at work in the world, and if you are comfortable, share the false narrative you see most at work in your own life.

3. "Sin is always ugly, and genuine virtue is always beautiful. Sin leads to ruin; virtue to greater strength. And this is why everyone, even atheists, love Jesus. Jesus was pure virtue. He lived a good and beautiful life, which he is calling his apprentices to live" (pp. 24-25). Describe in your own words what it means that Jesus lived a virtuous life.

4. "Narratives . . . try to guide us, to orient us, to tell us which way to turn" (p. 29). Can you think of a time in your life when one of your narratives was proven wrong? How did you work through this change? How is your life different now? How do your narratives compare to Jesus' narratives?

5. The author points out that we should not ask, "What will I have to give up to follow Jesus? but rather, What will I never get to experience if I choose not to follow Jesus?" (p. 31). What is your answer to the second question? Share it with the group.

ENGAGING SCRIPTURE [10-15 MINUTES]

Have a volunteer read aloud Matthew 7:24-27, then use the following discussion guide:

1. As a group name the different sources that have made up the foundation of your life and taught you how to be happy.

2. How has your foundation withstood the storms of life?

3. What resistance do you have toward Jesus' teachings: are they

too hard, too restrictive, outdated?

4. Pray as a group and invite Christ to be your sole (soul) foundation.

GO IN PEACE [5 MINUTES]
Conclude by having someone in your group read these words aloud.

> Each day, Jesus says to each of us, "Come, follow me." If we say yes, we can be sure that a good and beautiful day awaits us. And when we string those days together into months, years and decades, we will have lived a good and beautiful life. And that life is destined to echo a benediction of love for all of eternity to hear. (p. 32)

Go from your meeting with these words ringing in your ears! Amen.

NEXT WEEK
In chapter two we will explore Jesus' primary message about the kingdom of God. The soul-training exercise for the week will be play!

CHAPTER 2: THE GOSPEL MANY PEOPLE HAVE NEVER HEARD

OPENING TO GOD [5 MINUTES]
Begin with five minutes of silence followed by a brief prayer inviting God to guide the conversation.

SOUL TRAINING [10-15 MINUTES]
If you are in a group of six or more people, divide into groups of three or four. Use the following questions to help you process your experience of the soul-training exercise of play.

1. How did you play this week?

2. What surprised you as you attempted this practice? What challenged you?

3. What did you learn about God or yourself through the exercise?

ENGAGING THE CHAPTER [25-45 MINUTES]
Jesus' central teaching, his good news, is the availability of the kingdom of God.

1. Prior to reading this chapter, if someone asked you, "What is the gospel Jesus preached?" how would you have answered? How does your answer compare and contrast to the author's answer on page 35?

2. The author interprets "Repent, for the kingdom of heaven has come near" as "Change the way you have been thinking—a life of intimacy and interaction with God (the kingdom of God) is now in your midst" (p. 37). How does this interpretation differ from your own? How do you respond to the author's interpretation on both an intellectual and emotional level?

3. Why do you think the message of the kingdom of God has been lost in so many churches?

4. If you were having a conversation with a friend who said, "I believe the kingdom of God is *just* a promised future, not a present reality," what would you say to help him or her see it as *both* a future promise and a present reality? (For help check pp. 41-42, paragraph beginning "There is no doubt that the kingdom of God has not been fully established.")

5. The author speaks of the kingdom of God having "authority and power" (p. 43). Can you recall a time when you felt connected with a power outside of yourself that was good and loving? What happened? How did it feel? Although your story may seem odd or unusual, if you are comfortable share this experience with others in your group.

ENGAGING SCRIPTURE [15 MINUTES]
Have a volunteer in your group read aloud Luke 17:21-22. If members

of the group have different translations, you may want to note how they differ. Reflect on these questions:

1. How does this passage confirm the teaching of this chapter?

2. Review the author's definition of the kingdom of God (p. 42). With that definition in mind discuss what Jesus might mean when he says, "the kingdom of God is among you."

3. Spend five minutes in silence with your eyes closed. Breathe deeply and meditate on the fact that the kingdom of God is among your group right now. When the five minutes have passed, share with each other how it felt to ponder this beautiful truth.

GO IN PEACE [5 MINUTES]

Conclude by having one person in your group read aloud these words from the chapter.

> Change the way you have been thinking—a life of intimacy and interaction with God is now in your midst. (p. 37)

NEXT WEEK

In chapter three we explore the inclusivity of God's kingdom. The soul-training exercise for the week will be hospitality, so make plans early in the week to be hospitable.

CHAPTER 3: THE GRAND INVITATION

OPENING TO GOD [5 MINUTES]

Begin with five minutes of silence followed by a prayer inviting the Spirit of God to open your hearts.

SOUL TRAINING [10-15 MINUTES]

If you are in a group of six or more people, divide into groups of three or four. Use the following questions to help you process your soul-training experience.

1. Were you able to practice any of the suggestions for hospitality this week? If so, which ones?

2. What did you learn about God's presence in the lives of those who are different from you?

3. What did you learn about God or yourself through the exercises?

ENGAGING THE CHAPTER [25-45 MINUTES]

The Beatitudes are not prescriptions for blessedness but descriptions of the kinds of people who are invited to the kingdom.

1. The author opened the chapter with a beautiful story of Kevin and his testimony. What was your reaction to the story of Kevin's testimony?

2. Take a few moments to review the section "Jesus' Narrative: The Beatitudes Are Invitations of Inclusion," including the author's interpretation of the Beatitudes (pp. 55-62). Compare and contrast the author's interpretation with what you have been taught about the Beatitudes.

3. In discussing Luke 6:20-26, the author says, "Jesus' stern warning is born of love. He knows that we try to find solace in our wealth and fulfillment in our bellies. And we confuse fleeting pleasure with joy. When all is well in the kingdom of this world, we are tempted to think we have no need of the kingdom of God" (p. 63). Can you identify times when success led you away from or difficulties drew you closer to God? If you are comfortable, discuss these with the group.

4. Near the end of the chapter, the author reflects, "When I heard Kevin speak in church I was watching a *living beatitude*. His condition seemed unblessable in the kingdom of this world. According to society's values, he has nothing going for him. He is marginal-

ized, ostracized and neglected. No one would choose his situation. And yet he is welcomed, esteemed and valued in God's kingdom, which is why he smiled" (pp. 64-65). Have you known someone who is a "living beatitude"? If so, describe this person to your small group.

ENGAGING SCRIPTURE [15 MINUTES]

Have someone in your group read aloud Luke 6:20-26.

1. We may not think of people being in or out of the kingdom of God on a daily basis, but we often think of people being blessed and cursed because of their abilities and circumstances. Spend a few minutes brainstorming two lists in your group: one of those who are blessed from the *world's* perspective and the other of those who are cursed from the *world's* perspective.

2. After you have created your lists, consider how Jesus' message of God's inclusion affects the lives of those on both lists. Be as specific as possible.

3. Discuss how we, the followers of Jesus, can live out the message of invitation to those on *both* lists.

4. Conclude by reading aloud Luke 6:20-26 once again.

GO IN PEACE [5 MINUTES]

Conclude by having one person in your group read aloud these words.

Go from this place trusting that as you discover your identity as being indwelt by Christ, you will be empowered to live as a beatitude: a walking, talking, blessing to the world.

NEXT WEEK

In chapter four we will explore how living in the kingdom is the cure for anger. The soul-training exercise will be keeping a sabbath, so you will need to read the chapter early in the week and make necessary adjustments to your calendar.

CHAPTER 4: LEARNING TO LIVE WITHOUT ANGER

OPENING TO GOD [5 MINUTES]
Begin with five minutes of silence followed by a brief prayer inviting God's kingdom to be revealed to your group.

SOUL TRAINING [10-15 MINUTES]
If you are in a group of six or more people, divide into groups of three or four. Use the following questions to help you process your experience of the soul-training exercise of sabbath keeping.

1. Were you able to observe a sabbath this week? If so, describe what you did and how you felt about it. Remember it is acceptable to start small!

2. Were you able to experience a connection between sabbath and anger? If so, how are they related for you?

3. What did you learn about God or yourself from your sabbath rest?

ENGAGING THE CHAPTER [25-45 MINUTES]
The main idea of this chapter is that anger is caused by unmet expectations mixed with fear.

1. This chapter opens with the author's honest account of getting angry during a trip. What aspects of the author's story can you relate to?

2. The author gives us multiple "false imperative narratives" (FINs) (p. 73). Which FIN is most common in your life? How does it lead you to anger?

3. "Jesus' narrative is that God permits nothing to happen to us that

he cannot redeem and use for good. In the kingdom of heaven God is always near. We are never alone and never need to be afraid. When I live with this reality deep in my mind and heart, anger cannot get a grip on me" (p. 77). Do you have any evidence in your life of anger diminishing as you come to know that God is near to us and working for our good? If so and you are comfortable doing so, describe your experience to the group.

4. In the chapter we read this definition for righteous anger: "Righteous anger consists in getting angry at the things that anger God, and then seeking a proper remedy to correct the wrong" (p. 78). Give examples of righteous anger in today's world.

ENGAGING SCRIPTURE [15 MINUTES]

Have a volunteer in the group read aloud Galatians 5:16-17.

Have a second volunteer read this quote from the chapter:

> Many people assume that *flesh* refers to the body. But the "flesh" here is not the physical body but rather living from one's own resources in opposition to (or at least neglect of) God and his resources. The early church preacher John Chrysostom wrote, "The flesh is not the body, nor the essence of the body, but an evil disposition." There is a disposition within us that is prone to wander from God, and when we roam, we are "walking in the flesh." Those who live (or walk) in the flesh rely on their own capacity to solve problems. (p. 74)

1. Name examples from your own life when you relied on the Spirit rather than your own resources to do what God desired.

2. How does walking in the flesh versus walking in the Spirit impact your understanding of following Jesus?

GO IN PEACE [5 MINUTES]

Conclude by having someone in your group read these words aloud.

We may lose sight of God, but God never loses sight of us. God gives us space to experiment, grow and mature; God never intrudes. But this doesn't mean God is not with us, is not watching us, is not intimately familiar with our comings and goings. Jesus promised: "I will never leave you or forsake you." (p. 77)

NEXT WEEK

In chapter five we will see how living in the kingdom is the cure for lust. The soul-training exercise is a forty-eight-hour media fast. Again, you will need to make arrangements early in your week to observe this practice.

CHAPTER 5: LEARNING TO LIVE WITHOUT LUST

OPENING TO GOD [5 MINUTES]

Begin with five minutes of silence followed by a prayer inviting God's Spirit to work in your hearts through this material and discussion.

SOUL TRAINING [10-15 MINUTES]

If you are in a group of six or more people, divide into groups of three or four. Use the following questions to help you process your experience of fasting from media.

1. Were you able to fast from media this week? If so, describe what you did and how it felt.

2. What connections were you able to see between the media fast and lust?

3. What did you learn about God or yourself from the media fast?

ENGAGING THE CHAPTER [25-45 MINUTES]

The main idea of this chapter is that lust (*epithumia*) is the creation of a false image or persona. We objectify that persona or image in an attempt to fill a deep need for intimacy, which can only be met by our union with God in his kingdom.

1. What messages have you heard at church about sex? What has been implied about sex through silence?

2. On pages 91-92 the author connects *epithumia* and adultery, and he notes that in both cases, "valuing the other as a sacred being is tossed aside." Do you agree or disagree with the comparison between lust and adultery? If you are comfortable, explain.

3. The author discusses "*epithumia* for women" on pages 92-93. In what ways do you agree or disagree with the author's observations?

4. Near the end of the chapter, the author makes several points about how living in the kingdom of God is the cure for lust:

   • "In the kingdom we know who we are and whose we are. The need to feel loved, to be important, and to be sacred and special is met in our oneness with Christ." (p. 95)

   • "When I set my heart on things above (the kingdom) I discover that I am part of something thrilling and exciting—the divine conspiracy—and everywhere I turn God is at work. Now I have the drama I seek and I have a place to channel my energies." (p. 95)

   • "Finally, because I know who I am and am secure (God is good and desires my good) I am free to see others in a new way. I no longer see them as objects to exploit but as real persons who God dearly loves." (p. 95)

   How have your own experiences and struggles with lust affirmed or contradicted the points the author makes?

5. What is your reaction to the triangle of appropriate physical intimacy (p. 96)?

ENGAGING SCRIPTURE [15 MINUTES]

Have a volunteer in your group read aloud Colossians 3:1-11. Compare this Scripture with the points previously laid out in question 4. What correlation do you see? What does the writer of Colossians add to this process of transformation?

GO IN PEACE [5 MINUTES]

Conclude by having someone read the following quote:

> The process of metanoia is not merely a process of growing into a list of dos and don'ts, but rather an increasing recognition that you have earned nothing that you have—not your life or your body, not grace, not salvation. It is a process of learning to live thankfully (or, if you will, eucharistically)." (Lauren Winner, *Real Sex* [Grand Rapids: Brazos, 2005], p. 159)

NEXT WEEK

In chapter six we will explore how living in the kingdom is the cure for lying. The soul-training exercise for the week will be a day without words.

CHAPTER 6: LEARNING TO LIVE WITHOUT LYING

OPENING TO GOD [5 MINUTES]

Begin with five minutes of silence followed by a brief prayer inviting God's kingdom to be revealed to the deepest places of your heart.

SOUL TRAINING [10-20 MINUTES]

If you are in a group of six or more people, divide into groups of three or four. Use the following questions to help you process your experiences of going a day without words and without lying.

1. Which of the two exercises were you able to do this week? Describe what you did and how it felt.

2. What did you learn about God or yourself from the exercises?

3. Spend a few minutes reflecting on the soul-training exercises that have been covered in previous chapters. Which disciplines are you still practicing? How are they affecting you?

ENGAGING THE CHAPTER [30-45 MINUTES]

The main idea of this chapter is that we lie when disconnected to the kingdom and are unsure of our protection, identity and care, but in the kingdom we can dispense with lying.

1. The author gives an insightful list of lies we often tell:

   - Yes, I have read that book (or seen that movie).

   - Yes, let's definitely get together soon.

   - He's in a meeting.

   - She's not home.

   - No, that outfit doesn't make you look fat.

   As a group, add to this list by brainstorming lies we tell that seem harmless.

2. Two motives are given for lying: "in order to get what we want" or "to avoid something we don't want" (p. 108). If you are comfortable, discuss with the group which of these motives is most common for you. Are there other motives you would add?

3. In discussing Jesus' narrative about lying the author contrasts the "old law" with Jesus' teaching. He writes, "The standard of righteousness in Jesus' day was clear: You can tell lies and not be liable (until you get caught), but if you lie 'under oath' you are guilty. Jesus, as always, is aiming for something higher, for a new kind of person with a new kind of character. He is saying, 'Under oath or not, those who live in the kingdom can and should tell the truth'" (p. 110). Put an X on the continuum to represent where you think the average person stands regarding lying. Then

draw a circle for where you see yourself. Explain the locations of
the marks.

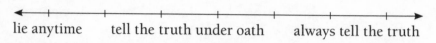

lie anytime   tell the truth under oath   always tell the truth

4. Have volunteers take turns reading aloud the first five paragraphs
   from the section titled "How Living in the Kingdom Can Cure Lying" on pages 112-13. Note the ways the kingdom of God sets us
   free from lying. As a group, discuss how your experiences of God's
   kingdom have reduced lying in your life.

ENGAGING SCRIPTURE [10-15 MINUTES]

Have one person in the group read aloud Colossians 3:9-10. In this
passage, Paul refers to the "new self," which can be seen as indwelt
by Christ and as residing in God's kingdom. The "old self," which
Paul invites us to take off, is isolated from God and God's resources.
As we put on the new self, lying is less necessary and less attractive
because of who we are and where we are.

1. How does living in God's kingdom and being indwelt by Christ
   affect the necessity and attractiveness of lying?

2. What soul-training exercises have helped you to take off your "old
   self" and put on the "new self" that Paul speaks of?

GO IN PEACE [5 MINUTES]

Conclude by having someone in your group pray aloud this verse:

> Let the words of my mouth and the meditation of my heart
>   be acceptable to you,
>   O LORD, my rock and my redeemer. (Psalm 19:14)

NEXT WEEK

In chapter seven we will see how living in the kingdom enables us to
bless those who curse us. The soul-training exercise for the week
will be praying for our competitors.

CHAPTER 7: LEARNING TO BLESS THOSE WHO CURSE US

OPENING TO GOD [5 MINUTES]

Begin with five minutes of silence followed by a brief prayer for God's wisdom and peace to work within your group.

SOUL TRAINING [10-20 MINUTES]

If you are in a group of six or more people, divide into groups of three or four. Use the following questions to discuss your experience of praying for the success of your competitors.

1. What did you notice happening within you and around you as you prayed for the success of your competitors?

2. What did you learn about God or yourself from the exercise?

ENGAGING THE CHAPTER [30-45 MINUTES]

The main idea of this chapter is that in the kingdom of God we are able to reach for something higher than retaliation and justice, and actually bless people who would harm us—just as Jesus did.

1. When the author's friend lost her job as a basketball coach, he gave her these words of truth: "Just remember, Jane, the kingdom is not in trouble, and Jane is not in trouble" (p. 120). When your life has been thrown into turmoil, how would these words have helped you?

2. In the section titled "Kingdom Jujitsu," the author explores the four teachings of Matthew 5:38-42. With this section in mind, discuss these questions.

   a. How does understanding Jesus' cultural context change your understanding of Matthew 5:38-42?

   b. The author discourages us from turning these teachings into law. Why is it tempting to make them into laws?

c. How does living in God's kingdom make it possible to follow this teaching?

3. What struck you when you read the section titled "Love Your Enemies"?

4. Miroslav Volf describes the person indwelt by Christ as "a rich self" and writes,

> A rich self looks toward the future with trust. It gives rather than holding things back in fear of coming out too short, because it believes God's promise that God will take care of it. Finite and endangered, a rich self still gives, because its life is "hidden with Christ" in the infinite, unassailable, and utterly generous God, the Lord of the present, the past, and the future. (p. 129)

With a partner, describe in your own words why the one indwelt by Christ is a "rich self."

5. Return to the three stories of those who dared to be extraordinary (pp. 130-32). What wisdom do you gain from their stories? What situations in your own life need this type of daring?

ENGAGING SCRIPTURE [10-15 MINUTES]

Have one person in the group read aloud Matthew 5:38-48. Jesus gives specific situations as well as ways kingdom-dwellers would respond. The author notes, "Kingdom *identity* (I am one in who Christ dwells) and kingdom *awareness* (I am in the strong and secure kingdom of God) are the keys to doing what Jesus calls us to do. With these we can learn how to become radically generous and to live extraordinary lives" (p. 130).

As a group, create three or four modern examples of the situations Jesus describes and how the follower of Christ might respond.

GO IN PEACE [5 MINUTES]

Conclude by having someone in your group read aloud this Dallas Willard quote:

> We know that we will be taken care of, no matter what. We can be vulnerable because we are, in the end, simply invulnerable. And once we have broken the power of anger and desire over our lives, we know that the way of Christ in response to personal injury and imposition is always the easier way. It is the only way that allows us to move serenely in the midst of the harm and beyond it. (p. 134)

NEXT WEEK

In chapter eight we will be exploring vainglory. The soul-training exercise for the week will be five acts of serving in secret. You will want to read the chapter early so you have plenty of opportunities to serve.

CHAPTER 8: LEARNING TO LIVE WITHOUT VAINGLORY

OPENING TO GOD [5 MINUTES]

Begin with five minutes of silence followed by a brief prayer inviting the Holy Spirit to reveal God's love to the group.

SOUL TRAINING [10-20 MINUTES]

If you are in a group of six or more people, divide into groups of three or four. Use the questions below to discuss your experience of serving in secret.

1. What was the most challenging aspect of serving in secret?

2. How did you feel as you were doing your secret acts of service? How did you feel *after* they were finished?

3. What, if anything, did you learn about God or yourself from the exercise?

ENGAGING THE CHAPTER [30-45 MINUTES]

The main idea of this chapter is that vainglory is the need to be thought well of by others; it is driven by the notion that the opinions of others determines our worth; when this vice is fully grown in our hearts we find ourselves more interested in others' opinions of us than actually being a genuinely good person or doing good for the sake of doing good.

Read through the following questions before you begin discussion. Note any questions you especially want to discuss. Depending on your group size and the conversation, you may not have time to discuss all the questions.

1. The author writes, "The world measures our worth on the basis of our appearance, production and performance—which seem to be the only thing that counts. This narrative says, Your value is determined by others' assessment" (p. 139). With a partner, discuss ways you allow your value to be determined by others.

2. Have you ever caught yourself doing some good deed not for the sake of helping others but for the prize of praise? If you are comfortable, talk about it with your group.

3. The author gives us this great insight into Jesus' teaching:

   Giving money to the poor. Praying. Fasting. All three activities are some of the most spiritual activities a person can do. So what about Jesus' harsh words? Actually, he is not speaking against these *practices*. He is attacking the way in which they are *being practiced*. He is not concerned about the *method* but the *motive*. As we have seen, Jesus starts with the world's standard of rightness (not murdering, not lying under oath) and then peels off the veneer to see if the heart is good. The same is true here. He takes three righteous and holy actions and then shows how the condition of a person's heart determines whether the discipline is a blessing or a hindrance. (pp. 144-45)

To explore your own motives, individually write down your three favorite spiritual practices. Consider your heart regarding these things.

- Do you long for approval and praise through any of these practices?

- Based on this chapter, what could you do to purify your motives regarding these disciplines?

- How could you apply the Puritan saying to "live for an audience of One" to your spiritual practices?

If you are comfortable, discuss your insights with the group.

ENGAGING SCRIPTURE [10-15 MINUTES]

The author writes, "No matter how many worldly 'trophies'" we acquire, we won't be able to lay our head down in peace because we are only as good as our last success. But our loving Father—the only One who matters—tells us that we are loved, that we are of immeasurable worth" (pp. 148-49). Using the steps below, prayerfully read 1 John 4:16-17 as a way to encounter God's love for you.

1. Have a volunteer read aloud 1 John 4:16-17. Simply hear the words and spend a minute in silence following the reading.

2. Have a second volunteer slowly read 1 John 4:16-17 again. As you listen to the passage, pay attention to any word or phrase that resonates in the deepest places of your heart. Repeat this word or phrase to yourself during a few minutes of silence.

3. Have a final volunteer read the passage once more. When the reading is over, spend seven to eight minutes in silent conversation with God. Give thanks, share concerns or just listen. Savor this time of being with God.

4. End the silence by having someone in the group say a prayer, or simply say "Amen."

GO IN PEACE [5 MINUTES]

Conclude by having one person in your group say this prayer, which is attributed to St. Francis of Assisi:

> O divine Master, grant that I might seek
> not so much to be consoled, as to console;
> to be understood, as to understand;
> and not so much to be loved, as to love another.
> Amen

NEXT WEEK

In the next chapter we will discover how living in the kingdom is the cure for avarice. The soul-training practice for the week is de-accumulation.

CHAPTER 9: LEARNING TO LIVE WITHOUT AVARICE

OPENING TO GOD [5 MINUTES]

Begin with five minutes of silence followed by a brief prayer inviting the Holy Spirit to lead you and your group into perfect freedom.

SOUL TRAINING [10-20 MINUTES]

If you are in a group of six or more people, divide into groups of three or four. Use the following questions to discuss your experience of deaccumulation.

1. What challenges did you encounter as you gave away some of your possessions?

2. How did it feel after you gave the items away?

3. What did you learn about God or yourself from the exercise?

ENGAGING THE CHAPTER [30-45 MINUTES]

The main idea of this chapter is that we are all stewards of the money we earn or are given, and we can invest them in either earthly or heavenly treasures.

1. At the beginning of the chapter the author shares his story of buying a pair of Adidas Americanas. With your group recount a possession you desperately wanted and eventually bought. How did you feel once you owned it? What finally happened to the item?

2. We read Suze Orman's story of watching her father save the cash register from a burning building and how it formed an important narrative for her (p. 156). With one or two people from your group, tell a story from your childhood that explains your view of money.

3. Have someone in the group read the following summary of Matthew 6:19-24:

   There are two types of treasures we can invest in (heavenly or earthly), two kinds of eyes (generous or stingy) and two deities we can serve (God or mammon). Earthly treasures are temporal; heavenly treasures are eternal. The wise choice is obvious. Stingy people are inwardly focused and don't experience joy; generous people are outwardly focused, give freely and experience joy. Giving is the wise choice. Finally, mammon says it can produce peace and happiness, but it fails. God promises peace and happiness, and always delivers. Who will we give our allegiance to? Our loving, giving, endlessly able Father. Jesus is not trying to shame us but is offering good investment advice. And that is because he understands the nature of the kingdom of God. (p. 161)

   What insights and questions do you have about this quote and Matthew 6:19-24?

4. The author gives us a story to help illustrate kingdom economics, about a time when he loaned money to an acquaintance (p. 162). If kingdom economics are real, how will you live differently after reading this chapter? As a group, brainstorm ways you can put

into practice kingdom economics. Let it be a joyful experiment and see what God does!

ENGAGING SCRIPTURE [10-15 MINUTES]

First Timothy 6:6-10 is a great passage to reflect on. The author says "Paul advocates contentment with adequate provisions. Beyond that we are tempted to serve mammon and not God" (p. 167).

Have a volunteer read 1 Timothy 6:6-10 aloud.

1. What strikes you about this Scripture passage?

2. What soul-training exercises have helped you develop the inner reality of contentment and simplicity?

3. What evidence do you have from your life that the desire to be rich leads to temptation?

GO IN PEACE [5 MINUTES]

Close your time together by having someone in the group read these valuable words:

> Treasures in heaven relate to the things God is doing. And we know that God is helping people. Thus the best way to lay up treasures in heaven is to live out Matthew 6:33: "Seek ye first the kingdom of God, and his righteousness, and all these things shall be added unto you" (KJV). (p. 159)

NEXT WEEK

In chapter ten we will explore how living in the kingdom is the cure for worry. The soul-training exercise for the week is a specific form of prayer. It will be best to engage in this prayer throughout the entire week.

CHAPTER 10: LEARNING TO LIVE WITHOUT WORRY

OPENING TO GOD [5 MINUTES]

Begin with five minutes of silence followed by a brief prayer inviting the Holy Spirit to lead you and your group deeper into God's kingdom.

SOUL TRAINING [10-20 MINUTES]

If you are in a group of six or more people, divide into groups of three or four. The soul-training exercise for the week was prayer. Regarding the relationship between prayer and worry, the author says,

> God has instituted prayer as one of his means of caring for us. We are invited to turn our cares into prayers. And when we do, we put the matter into God's hands. This does not take away our responsibility in dealing with our concerns, but it places the concerns in the larger context of the kingdom. It allows God to use the resources of the kingdom to meet our needs. When we do this, Paul says, we discover a peace that surpasses our understanding. (p. 180)

Use the following questions to discuss your experience of prayer.

1. In what ways did you see the kingdom of God at work in the areas you prayed about?

2. Did you find greater peace as you offered these prayers? If so, how did it affect you?

3. What did you learn about God or yourself from the exercise?

ENGAGING THE CHAPTER [30-45 MINUTES]

The main idea of this chapter is that people who live in the kingdom of God never need to worry about their lives.

1. The author differentiates worry and caution. Describe the difference.

2. In this chapter we explore the relationship between the media and our fears. Reflect for a few minutes on the news media you consume. What fears do they play on? How does the media influence your awareness and openness to God's kingdom? Discuss these

questions with two other people in your group.

3. Review the section titled "Jesus' Narrative: Things Not to Worry About" (pp. 175-78). As a group reflect on the various points from this section that you find either challenging or helpful.

4. Commentators Dale C. Allison and W. D. Davies note that "anxiety is foolish and accomplishes nothing except to put God out of the picture" (p. 179). Do you agree with this statement? Explain. Why are the kingdom of God and anxiety mutually exclusive?

5. In discussing Matthew 6:34, the author writes,

> Jesus says that the kingdom operates only in the present moment. We can only live in the kingdom today. We can't live in it tomorrow. So worrying about tomorrow is a useless distraction. Just as we count on God today, we can count on him tomorrow. But we aren't in tomorrow, and never will be; we live only in the present, in *today*. (p. 180)

How does this differ from our culture's typical notion regarding tomorrow?

ENGAGING SCRIPTURE [10-15 MINUTES]

The author tells us that Matthew 6:33 "is the key to the entire Sermon on the Mount" (p. 178). Go to section "One Day at a Time" (pp. 180-81), and highlight points that are especially helpful or challenging to you. Once everyone has had a chance to discuss, prayerfully engage Matthew 6:33 using the following steps.

1. Have each person read the verse aloud, slowly. Leave a brief pause between each reading.

2. Once everyone has read the verse, spend five to ten minutes in silence, reflecting on the passage and what practical steps you can take to seek first God's kingdom.

3. Allow time for anyone in the group to share their insights from this time of silence.

GO IN PEACE [5 MINUTES]
Close your time together by having someone in the group read this quote:

> As long as we live in fellowship with our good and beautiful God in his mighty kingdom, we have nothing to fear, not even fear itself. For nothing in life or death can separate us from the love of God (Romans 8:38-39). When we know this to be true, we can let go of worry and begin living with confidence and joy. (p. 182)

NEXT WEEK
In chapter eleven we will discover how living in the kingdom is the cure for judging others. The soul-training exercise is to go an entire day without gossip.

CHAPTER 11: LEARNING TO LIVE WITHOUT JUDGING OTHERS

OPENING TO GOD [5 MINUTES]
Begin with five minutes of silence followed by a brief prayer asking the Spirit of Christ to keep teaching you new ways of living.

SOUL TRAINING [10-15 MINUTES]
If you are in a group of six or more people, divide into groups of three or four. Use the following questions to discuss your experience of going a day without gossiping.

1. What struggles did you discover when you couldn't gossip?

2. How did your perspective of other people change during this exercise?

3. What did you learn about God or yourself from the exercise?

ENGAGING THE CHAPTER [30-45 MINUTES]

The main idea of this chapter is that judging others is a common way we try to control them, but it fails. Jesus' method is to pray for, to ask, to seek and to stand with those we want to see change.

1. The author summarizes this way why judging fails: "Condemnation engineering fails because it doesn't come across as loving, it doesn't allow the person to own the need for change, it doesn't offer help toward change, and it may be entirely inaccurate" (p. 190). What would you add to or remove from this list of condemnation engineering flaws? Why?

2. Do you have family members who have used condemnation engineering on you? If so, what was the result?

3. The author takes a different approach to Matthew 7:7-11's ask, seek and knock (p. 193)? What is your reaction to his interpretation?

4. The author tells us that judging others comes from a desire to change others or a need to feel better about ourselves as beloved by God and living within God's kingdom. Have there been times you felt more connected to the kingdom of God and as a result were less judgmental? If so, discuss these experiences with the group.

ENGAGING SCRIPTURE [10-15 MINUTES]

Have a volunteer read John 8:1-11, then discuss these questions as a group:

1. What stated and unstated motivations did the Pharisees have for judging this woman?

2. Imagine yourself in the place of the woman caught in adultery. How might this experience change you?

3. What wisdom and encouragement can we gain from this Bible

story when it comes to our relationships with people that we want to change?

GO IN PEACE [5 MINUTES]

The author finishes the chapter by reflecting on the situation with his son. Close your time together by having someone in the group read this paragraph aloud:

> If we really want to see people change, we have to be willing to come alongside and participate with them, to make sacrifices of our own time and energy. I am so thankful that I have the privilege of prayer and the resources of the kingdom of God. Even if Jacob's problem had not been solved, it still would have been a great blessing. We learned about doing the hard work required of all life's endeavors, and in the process my son and I grew closer. Building your life on the commands of Jesus, though sometimes challenging, is building on a solid foundation. (pp. 200-201)

NEXT WEEK

In chapter twelve we will explore how living in the kingdom is a way of life. The soul-training exercise for the week is to live a day devotionally. You may want to observe this practice for several days, so read the chapter early to give yourself time to try it.

CHAPTER 12: LIVING IN THE KINGDOM DAY BY DAY

OPENING TO GOD [5 MINUTES]

Begin with five minutes of silence followed by a brief prayer inviting Christ to guide the group into his way of life.

SOUL TRAINING [10-15 MINUTES]

If you are in a group of six or more people, divide into groups of three or four. Use the following questions to discuss your experience of living one day (or more) devotionally.

1. What changes did you have to make in your daily routine to follow Madame Guyon's rule?

2. What changes would you make to this daily rule to continue living it?

3. What did you learn about God or yourself from the exercise?

ENGAGING THE CHAPTER [30-45 MINUTES]

The main idea of this chapter is that we cannot live an effective and joyful Christian life if we do not practice spiritual disciplines.

1. At the beginning of the chapter the author compares caring for his devotional life to tending a fire. What is your reaction to this illustration?

2. This chapter addresses two false narratives: (1) "What matters is having faith in Jesus, not having an ongoing relationship with him," and (2) "The only way to be a good Christian is to keep all the rules" (pp. 206-7). How have these narratives shaped your own faith journey?

3. In explaining John 15:5-8 the author writes, "To abide in Christ involves spending time with Jesus. For me, this happens when I keep my mind and my heart set on his presence with me" (p. 209). What practices help you to abide in Christ? What impact does this have on your life?

4. Of the four images Jesus gives at the end of the Sermon on the Mount (wide vs. narrow gate, inner vs. outer reality, people claiming to know Jesus but don't; and building on sand vs. rock) (pp. 210-13), which one is the most challenging to you? Why?

5. As you grow in seeing yourself as being indwelt by Christ and living in the unshakeable kingdom of God, have you been able to endure life's storms differently? Describe the difference.

ENGAGING SCRIPTURE [10-15 MINUTES]

Have a group member read Matthew 7:24-27 aloud, then discuss these questions as a group:

1. If you were explaining this passage to a friend, what would you tell him or her?

2. Given what you have learned from this book, what steps can you take in the days ahead to build your spiritual house on the solid foundation of Christ's teachings?

GO IN PEACE [5 MINUTES]

Close your time together by having someone in the group read this paragraph:

> The only way to nurture my relationship with Jesus is to set my heart and mind on the kingdom of God. The fundamental building block of an apprentice of Jesus is living closely to Jesus in our ordinary lives. If we can learn how to spend an ordinary day with our minds set on things above we will have learned one of the most important spiritual exercises in the Christian life. (p. 214)

LOOKING FORWARD

Your study of *The Good and Beautiful Life* has come to an end, but there are many options for your group. One is to begin the next book in the Apprentice Series, *The Good and Beautiful Community*, which explores how we can live as apprentices of Jesus in our everyday lives.

Another option is for members of the current group to form new groups and invite their friends to go through *The Good and Beautiful God* together, which is the first book in this series. This would be a great way to continue "pickling" in these narratives and falling more deeply in love with God. Whatever you decide, select a date for your group to begin.

Notes

Introduction

p. 9   "You ask, what would I do with them?": John Wesley, taken from no. 19 of "An Earnest Appeal to Men of Reason and Religion," *The Works of John Wesley: On Compact Disc* (Franklin, Tenn.: Providence House, 1995).

Chapter 1: The Good and Beautiful Life

p. 19   Eighty-five percent said happiness: J. P. Moreland and Klaus Issler, *The Lost Virtue of Happiness* (Colorado Springs: NavPress, 2006), p. 16.

p. 22   God's wrath is his righteous stand against sin: For more on God's wrath, read chap. 6, "God Is Holy," in *The Good and Beautiful God* (Downers Grove, Ill.: InterVarsity Press, 2009).

p. 24   "Without [virtue] there can be no happiness": Thomas Merton, *The Seven Storey Mountain* (New York: Harcourt, 1948), p. 223.

p. 26   "Discipline yourself so others won't have to": See Jay Carty and John Wooden, *Coach Wooden One on One* (Ventura, Calif.: Regal, 2003).

p. 29   "if the map don't agree with the ground": Gordon Livingston, *Too Soon Old, Too Late Smart* (New York: Marlowe, 2004), pp. 1-2.

p. 30   "God cannot give us a happiness and peace apart from himself": C. S. Lewis, *Mere Christianity* (New York: Macmillan, 1952), p. 54.

p. 31   "Nondiscipleship costs abiding peace": Dallas Willard, quoted in James Bryan Smith and Richard J. Foster, *Devotional Classics* (San Francisco: HarperSanFrancisco, 1992), p. 6.

Chapter 2: The Gospel Many People Have Never Heard

p. 37   The kingdom of God (or kingdom of the heaven): Kingdom of God and kingdom of heaven are synonymous. Matthew uses the latter, scholars think, because he was writing to a Jewish audience, who would have been uncomfortable using the sacred name of God.

p. 40   Dallas Willard recounts the following: Dallas Willard, quoted in James Bryan Smith and Richard J. Foster, *Devotional Classics* (San Francisco: HarperSanFrancisco, 1992), p. 59.

p. 40   Martyn Lloyd-Jones, the great British preacher: Martyn Lloyd-Jones, *The Kingdom of God* (Wheaton, Ill.: Crossway, 1992), p. 8.

p. 41   "The New Testament church . . . was confident": John Bright, *The Kingdom of God* (Nashville: Abingdon, 1981), p. 244.

Chapter 3: The Grand Invitation

p. 55   "the cultically impure were welcomed at Jesus' table": L. Gregory Jones, *Embodying Forgiveness* (Grand Rapids: Eerdmans, 1995), p. 121.

p. 57   "the largeness of Christ's World-Kingdom": Alfred Edersheim, *The Life and Times of Jesus the Messiah* (Peabody, Mass.: Hendrickson, 1993), p. 367.

p. 57   Matthew's and Luke's versions of "Blessed are the poor": Matthew's and Luke's versions likely differ because of a linguistic problem. The word Jesus probably used (Jesus spoke in Aramaic) was the Aramaic word *in-wetan*, which is connected to the Hebrew word *anawim*. The word translated "poor in spirit" is *anawim* ("Blessed are the *anawim*"). *Anawim* "didn't mean 'destitute' but stood for a more complex concept that included a religious dimension." According to Anna Wierzbicka, there was no Greek word that could fully explain this concept, so Matthew used this word to denote that Jesus was referring not only to those who were poor monetarily (as in Luke's version) but those who were poor in other dimensions of life as well (*What Did Jesus Mean?* [Oxford: Oxford University Press, 2001], pp. 37-39).

p. 57   Dallas Willard's translation of "poor in spirit": Dallas Willard, *The Divine Conspiracy* (San Francisco: HarperSanFrancisco, 1998), p. 100. I also like Wierzbicka's statement about the *anawim*: "the little ones . . . are people who know that they cannot live if God doesn't do good things for them and who think at the same time that God can and wants to do good things for them" (Wierzbicka, *What Did Jesus Mean?* p. 39).

pp. 57-58   "those who were marginal to society or outcasts": Wierzbicka, *What Did Jesus Mean?* p. 38.

p. 58   a person "whose situation is wretched": R. T. France, *The Gospel of Matthew* (Grand Rapids: Eerdmans, 2007), p. 165.

p. 59   "the kingdom of the heavens enfolds them": Willard, *Divine Conspiracy,* p. 117.

p. 64   Pope Benedict XVI explains this beautifully: Pope Benedict XVI, *Jesus of Nazareth* (New York: Doubleday, 2007), pp. 71-72.

p. 66   "When we speak of hospitality": Daniel Homan and Lonni Collins Pratt, *Radical Hospitality* (Brewster, Mass.: Paraclete, 2002), p. 3.

p. 67   "Opening yourselves to the stranger": Ibid., p. 21.

p. 67   "She is the liberal if I am conservative": Ibid., p. 63.

p. 68   "You prepare for others when": Ibid., p. 117.

p. 68   "You can put down the phone and listen": Ibid., p. 43.

Chapter 4: Learning to Live Without Anger

p. 74   "The flesh is not the body": John Chrysostom, quoted in *The New Schaff-Herzog Encyclopedia of Religious Knowledge* (New York: Funk & Wagnalls, 1909), 3:329.

p. 77   "How do people change?": Andrew D. Lester, *The Angry Christian* (Louisville, Ky.: Westminster John Knox, 2003), pp. 100-101.

p. 78   "Righteous anger consists in getting angry": Neil T. Anderson and Rich
             Miller, *Getting Anger Under Control* (Eugene, Ore.: Harvest House, 2002),
             p. 54.

p. 79   "Paul is saying here that it is not the anger itself": Archibald Hart, *Feeling
             Free* (Old Tappan, N.J.: Revell, 1979), p. 74.

p. 81   "Sabbath rest is thus a call to Sabbath trust": Norman Wirzba, *Living the
             Sabbath* (Grand Rapids: Brazos, 2006), p. 38.

Chapter 5: Learning to Live Without Lust

p. 86   Over fourteen thousand sexual references: Lauren Winner, *Real Sex*
             (Grand Rapids: Brazos, 2005), p. 63.

p. 87   "The two main errors in the area of human sexuality": Dallas Willard,
             "Spirituality and Ministry," a D.Min. course at Fuller Theological Semi-
             nary I cotaught with Dallas for ten years.

p. 87   brilliant and influential writer Augustine of Hippo: There is debate
             about whether Augustine ought to be blamed for this narrative. He
             clearly had some negative views about sexuality. But given his cultural
             situation, some suggest he had a fairly balanced, even progressive, view
             of sexuality.

p. 95   "If it's just me against the lust": Rob Bell, *Sex God: Exploring the Endless
             Connections Between Sexuality and Spirituality* (Grand Rapids: Zondervan,
             2007), pp. 81-83.

p. 95   "Gratitude is so central to the life God made us for": Ibid., p. 74.

p. 95-98   Richard Foster's triangle diagram: The diagram appears in Richard Foster,
             The Challenge of the Disciplined Life (San Fransisco: HarperSanFrancisco,
             1989), p. 129

Chapter 6: Learning to Live Without Lying

p. 105   we tell an average of 3.3 lies: Ralph Keyes, *The Post-Truth Era* (New York:
             St. Martin's Press, 2004), p. 3.

p. 105   we are lied to every five minutes: I heard this on the August 27, 2007,
             Oprah Winfrey Show. It also was on the show's website, but gave no refer-
             ence for the study. I have not been able to find the original study.

p. 105   "some form of deception occurs in nearly two-thirds of all conversations":
             Keyes, *Post-Truth Era*, p. 7.

p. 105   59 percent of Americans parents admitted to lying: Ibid., p. 250.

p. 105   "nearly all of us tell lies, and far more often than we realize": Ibid., p. 7.

p. 105   Wealthy parents take their kids "diagnosis shopping": David Callahan,
             The Cheating Culture (Orlando: Harcourt, 2004), p. 8.

p. 105   "gross misinformation" on résumés: Keyes, *Post-Truth Era*, p. 63.

p. 105   Americans have illegal offshore bank accounts: Callahan, *Cheating Cul-
             ture*, p. 8.

p. 106   "stealing $6 billion a year worth of paid television": Ibid., p. 11.

p. 106   fraudulent practices at auto repair centers: Ibid., pp. 30-32.

p. 106   "Americans are not only cheating more": Ibid., p. 13.

p. 106   "excusing our lies": Keyes, *Post-Truth Era*, p. 8.

p. 112   "a false statement made knowingly, with the intent to deceive": Ibid., p.
                  9.

p. 114   "Radical Honesty": I first heard about this from an article in the July 2007
                  issue of *Esquire*.

Chapter 7: Learning to Bless Those Who Curse Us

p. 124   if a Roman soldier asked a Jew to carry his luggage: In Matthew 27:32 we
                  see an incidence of this when Simon is ordered by a Roman to carry the
                  cross.

p. 128   "[Jesus] chose the way of the cross": David Augsburger, *Dissident Disciple-
                  ship* (Grand Rapids: Brazos, 2006), p. 137.

p. 129   "more than enough people": Miroslav Volf, *Free of Charge* (Grand Rapids:
                  Zondervan, 2005), p. 109.

p. 129   "A rich self looks toward the future with trust": Ibid., p. 110.

p. 130   *Teleios* refers to spiritual maturity: R. T. France, *The Gospel of Matthew*
                  (Grand Rapids: Eerdmans, 2007), p. 228.

pp. 130-31   John Paul II and Mohammed Agca: Volf, *Free of Charge*, p. 171.

pp. 131   "Steven's son Bobby was killed in the September 11 attacks": Shane Clai-
                  borne, *The Irresistible Revolution* (Grand Rapids: Zondervan, 2006), pp.
                  204-5.

pp. 131-32   The mothers of Boyle Heights: Augsburger, *Dissident Discipleship*, p. 126.

p. 134   "We know that we will be taken care of": Dallas Willard, *The Divine Con-
                  spiracy* (San Francisco: HarperSanFrancisco, 1998), p. 181.

Chapter 8: Learning to Live Without Vainglory

pp. 140-41   John Cassian on vainglory: John Cassian, *The Monastic Institutes* (London:
                  Saint Austin Press, 1999), p. 163.

p. 141   "There is no pride so dangerous": Andrew Murray, *Humility* (Minneapolis:
                  Bethany House, 2001), p. 64.

p. 141   "This disease strikes precisely where a man's virtue lies": Cassian, *Monas-
                  tic Institutes*, pp. 163-65.

p. 144   "When someone gave a significant gift": R. T. France, *The Gospel of Mat-
                  thew*, New International Commentary on the New Testament (Grand Rap-
                  ids: Eerdmans, 2007) p. 236.

p. 146   "[God] is himself invisible": Ibid., p. 239.

p. 146   Why "must we pray?": John Chrysostom, "Homily 19 on St. Matthew: On
                  the Lord's Prayer," in Nicene and Post-Nicene Fathers, first series, vol. 10,
                  ed. Philip Schaff, trans. George Prevost and rev. M. B. Riddle (Buffalo,
                  N.Y.: Christian Literature Publishing, 1888). Rev. and ed. for New Advent

site by Kevin Knight <www.newadvent.org/fathers/200119.htm>.

p. 147   "The whole life of Jesus of Nazareth": Henri Nouwen, *The Selfless Way of Christ* (Maryknoll, N.Y.: Orbis, 2007), p. 31.

p. 148   John Calvin on contemplating the face of God: John Calvin, quoted in C. J. Mahaney, *Humility* (Colorado Springs: Multnomah Books, 2005), p. 21.

Chapter 9: Learning to Live Without Avarice

p. 154   "roughly ninety percent of our consumer buying": Martin Lindstrom, *Buyology* (New York: Doubleday, 2008), p. 195

p. 156   Suze Orman's story about her father: Suze Orman, *The 9 Steps to Financial Freedom* (New York: Crown, 1997), p. 3.

p. 157   "Just a little bit more": I have heard this story many times through the years but am unable to find a reference, which means it may be apocryphal.

p. 159   "We reveal what our treasures are by": Dallas Willard, *The Divine Conspiracy* (San Francisco: HarperSanFrancisco, 1998), pp. 203-4.

p. 159   "belonging to and living by the priorities": R. T. France, *Gospel of Matthew* (Grand Rapids: Eerdmans, 2007), p. 259.

p. 160   "unhealthy eye" referred to a stingy, envious, jealous person: Ibid., p. 262.

p. 160   "no record of *mammon* being used in a negative way": Ibid.

p. 161   wealth pretends to offers what we want from God: Wesley K. Willmer, *God and Your Stuff* (Colorado Springs: NavPress, 2002), p. 26.

p. 163   brain scans of people of faith: Lindstrom, *Buyology*, p. 108.

p. 164   powerful brands and religious experiences: Ibid., p. 124.

p. 164   watching ads for six straight years: Ibid., p. 37.

pp. 164-65   fear-driven advertising: Ibid., p. 138.

p. 166   simplicity is "an inward reality that results in an outward lifestyle": Richard J. Foster, *Celebration of Discipline* (San Francisco: HaperSanFrancisco, 1978), p. 69.

Chapter 10: Learning to Live Without Worry

p. 172   "The little freckle on your arm could be a time bomb": Adapted from Scott Bader-Saye, *Following Jesus in a Culture of Fear* (Grand Rapids: Brazos, 2007), p. 14.

p. 173   "fear for profit" syndrome: Ibid., p. 16.

p. 173   "Television news programs survive on scares": Barry Glassner, *The Culture of Fear* (New York: Basic Books, 1999), p. xxi.

pp. 176-77   "This novel twisting of an old motif": Dale C. Allison and W. D. Davies, *Commentary on Matthew VII-XVIII*, International Critical Commentary (Edinburgh: T & T Clark, 1991), p. 653.

p. 179   "Anxiety is foolish and accomplishes nothing": Ibid., p. 652.

Chapter 11: Learning to Live Without Judging Others

p. 188   condemnation engineering: "Condemnation Engineering" is a phrase I have heard often by Dallas Willard, so I must give him credit for this insightful term.

p. 192   I may be wrong, but I ask that you open your mind: Dallas Willard has shaped my interpretation of the Sermon on the Mount (see *The Divine Conspiracy*). It took me many years to agree with Dallas's teaching on the Sermon, but I have come to agree with his interpretation. Though Dallas is a philosopher and not a New Testament scholar, I believe he understands the Sermon on the Mount with greater clarity than any single scholar I have read.

p. 193   "Despite their arguments, I fully disagree": Dale C. Allison and W. D. Davies, as well as R. T. France hold that Jesus is here offering a corrective to his liberal teaching on not judging, namely, that there are cases where we would be wasting our time trying to help people who do not want our help. With all due respect, I disagree. The primary reason is that it goes against the grain of the Sermon. For example, Allison believes that Jesus is balancing his laxity toward judgment by warning people about offering the gospel to those who do not want to hear it—a moral symmetry. The kingdom of God is the pearl, he notes, and there are hardhearted people who are not worthy of it: "There has to be an economy of truth" (Dale C. Allison and W. D. Davies, *Commentary on Matthew VII-XVIII*, International Critical Commentary [Edinburgh: T & T Clark, 1991], pp. 674-76).

p. 197   "The whole business of judging persons": T. W. Manson, quoted in Allison and Davies, *Commentary on Matthew*, p. 669.

p. 198   "Do not unto another what you would not": John Wesley, "Sermon XXX: Upon Our Lord's Sermon on the Mount," *Sermons on Several Occasions*, vol. 1, ed. Thomas Jackson and Thomas Osmond Summers (New York: Carlton & Phillips, 1855), p. 285.

Chapter 12: Living in the Kingdom Day by Day

pp. 208-9   "to abide means to rest and rely on Jesus": James Bryan Smith, *The Good and Beautiful God* (Downers Grove, Ill.: InterVarsity Press, 2009), p. 159.

p. 210   "Nondiscipleship costs abiding peace": Dallas Willard, quoted in Richard Foster and James Bryan Smith, *Devotional Classics* (San Francisco: HarperSanFrancisco, 1992), p. 16.

p. 211   false prophets are not "heretics": John Chrysostom, "Homily 23.6, Matthew 7:16," *The Homilies of S. John Chrysostom on the Gospel of St. Matthew*, trans. George Prevost (Oxford: J. H. Parker, 1843), p. 356.

p. 211   we ought not "look to the mask": Quoted in *Matthew 1—13*, ed. Manlio Simonetti, Ancient Christian Commentary on Scripture (Downers Grove, Ill.: InterVarsity Press, 2001), p. 152.

pp. 216-17   "A Mother's Advice to Her Daughter": This translation comes from an excerpt in John Wesley's *A Christian Library*, and was modernized by James Bryan Smith and Danielle Howard.

p. 218 "Covenant Prayer": Quoted in Frank Whaling, ed., *John and Charles Wesley: Selected Prayers, Hymns, Journal Notes, Sermons, Letters and Treatises,* Classics of Western Spirituality (Mahwah, N.J.: Paulist Press, 1981), p. 59.

p. 220 "If you've got troubles and just can't sleep": Irving Berlin, "Count Your Blessings Instead of Sheep," 1954.

acknowledgments

This book—and all of the books in the Apprentice Series—would not exist were it not for Dallas Willard, a living example of a true apprentice of Jesus, who has inspired me in countless ways. Dallas's outline of a "curriculum for Christlikeness" is the framework of these books. It is difficult to measure the impact of his life and writings on my soul.

And these books would not have been written if it were not for Richard J. Foster, who has poured his life and wisdom into me for over twenty-five years. Everyone should have a teacher as brilliant and authentic as Richard—I am grateful. Thank you, Richard, for finding something in me worth believing in and taking a chance on.

The person who made the most sacrifice is my wonderful, beautiful, fun and very patient wife, Meghan Smith. She endured many months as a "writer's widow" and never complained. Thank you, Meghan, for knowing how important this series is to me by supporting and encouraging me every step of the way. And thanks for editing the material along the way. My whole life is better because of you. You still take my breath away.

My son and daughter, Jacob and Hope also gave up a lot as I wrote.

Thank you for allowing me to tell your stories. Thanks too for supporting me while I wrote, rewrote, edited and taught this material. I know that time spent with others is time taken from you. I will work to make it up to you!

I also want to thank my four former disciples and now colleagues for all the encouragement and support you have given me. Thanks to the two "sons of thunder": Patrick Sehl, for your relentless support of me and love for this material, and C. J. Fox, for being an example of integrity and enthusiasm; and to the two wise hobbits Matt Johnson, for your quiet confidence, dedication to the King and the kingdom, and scent of patchouli; and Jimmy Taylor, for your creativity and depth and sheer love of Jesus. These four young men are going to change the world.

I also want to thank three of my colleagues at Friends University who read the manuscripts of the Apprentice Series, offered a lot of helpful suggestions and helped me avoid some errors—Dr. Chris Ketter, for your theological insights, Dr. Stan Harstine, for your biblical brilliance, and Dr. Darcy Zabel for your literary skills.

I owe a great debt to Kathy Helmers, my agent and guide through the maze of publishing, for sharing my love for these books, shaping them into something good and then finding the right publishing partner. Kathy, you are the best at what you do, and I am fortunate to work with you.

Thanks to Jeff Crosby and Cindy Bunch of InterVarsity Press, who made it clear to me from the moment we met that you were quality people with incredible skills, a passion for publishing good books, and a clear vision for what this series is and can be. I am blessed to work with you both.

I also need to thank others who contributed in hidden ways:

Bob Casper—for your belief in me and these books and your brilliant mind.

Jeff Gannon—my pastor, friend and fellow worker in the kingdom.

Lyle SmithGraybeal—for never once doubting these books.

Vicki and Scott Price—for loving me and believing in these books.

Ashley Brockus—for encouragement and assistance so the work could get done.

Additionally, I wish to thank a few people that I neglected to acknowledge in the first book, and those people are: Jeff Noyes, Natalie Bryant and Jason Bryant.

Finally, thank you to the 109 people who went through this course at Chapel Hill United Methodist Church, Wichita, who studied and practiced the concepts in these books, and allowed me to learn from your experiences and insights. Your presence is felt in the pages of these books.

Be Inspired!

www.hodderfaith.com

Visit our new website for:

New books and Bibles releases

Author Q&As

Competitions

Extra Content

Bible Search function

Podcasts and author videos

News and events diary with interactive map

Links to ministry pages, author websites, live Twitter feeds

& much more

www.hodderfaith.com
Where Faith is Inspired

HODDER &
STOUGHTON

CBC Publisher of the Year 2008 & 2009

RENOVARÉ

www.renovare.org

Just over twenty years ago Richard J. Foster, my mentor and friend, said to me, "Jim, I'm starting a ministry. It is time for the walls to come down that separates denominations. The church needs to do better at its primary job—making disciples. And people need to learn how to practice the disciplines not just as individuals but within groups. We need to help the modern church connect to the ancient church. I'd like you to help me design it and help lead it." I said yes. A month later we met for lunch and Richard told me he had come up with a name for this spiritual renewal ministry: RENOVARÉ (ren-o-var-ay), a Latin word that means "to renew." I knew right away we were in trouble: no one could pronounce it, and no one knew what it meant. But it sounded really cool, because from the very start it was already doing what nobody else dared to

Most parachurch organizations set out to do what they think churches aren't doing on their own, but RENOVARÉ comes alongside churches and resources them without pretending to do their job, namely, making disciples of Jesus Christ. Unfortunately, people have separated the word *disciple* from discipline. They forget that the followers of Christ were *disciples* because they practiced the *disciplines* of Christ, and the disciples spiritual lives were made rich through the practices of prayer, morality, sharing the gospel, service, communion and spiritual gifts.

RENOVARÉ is helping us—individuals and churches—to overcome our forgetfulness and rediscover these practices, these disciplines, in order that we, like the first-century Christians, can know what it is to walk closely with Jesus and become more like him. I've worked with RENOVARÉ for all these years (and partnered with them in the development of this book series) because they know that following Christ goes beyond denominations, even beyond the latest church program, and gives us tools to discovering life with God in the very fabric of our everyday lives.

This book is very much a part of what RENOVARÉ is all about—it has the same DNA as RENOVARÉ. So I hope you don't stop here, because as an organization and a community of the most kind and Christlike people I know RENOVARÉ continues the conversation and the journey you have begun in this book. Come and walk with us.